P9-CRJ-914

MOMMYWOOD

ALSO BY TORI SPELLING

sTORI telling

MOMMYWOOD

TORI SPELLING

WITH HILARY LIFTIN

SIMON SPOTLIGHT ENTERTAINMENT
NEW YORK LONDON TORONTO SYDNEY

SSE

Simon Spotlight Entertainment
A Division of Simon & Schuster, Inc.
1230 Avenue of the Americas
New York, NY 10020

Copyright © 2009 by Tori Spelling

All rights reserved, including the right to reproduce this book or portions thereof
in any form whatsoever. For information address Pocket Books Subsidiary
Department, 1230 Avenue of the Americas, New York, NY 10020.

First Simon Spotlight Entertainment hardcover edition April 2009

SIMON SPOTLIGHT ENTERTAINMENT and colophon are trademarks of
Simon & Schuster, Inc.

Certain names and identifying characteristics have been changed.

All photos are from Tori Spelling's personal collection except where otherwise credited.

For information about special discounts for bulk purchases, please contact Simon
& Schuster Special Sales at 1-866-506-1949 or business@simonandschuster.com.

The Simon & Schuster Speakers Bureau can bring authors to your live event. For
more information or to book an event contact the Simon & Schuster Speakers
Bureau at 1-866-248-3049 or visit our website at www.simonspeakers.com.

Designed by Jaime Putorti

Manufactured in the United States of America

10 9 8 7 6 5 4 3 2 1

Library of Congress Cataloging-in-Publication Data

Spelling, Tori, 1973–
Mommywood : Tori Spelling with Hilary Liftin.
p. cm.
1. Spelling, Tori, 1973– 2. Actors—United States—Biography. 3. Motherhood—
United States—Biography. I. Liftin, Hilary. II. Title.
PN2287.S664A3 2009
791.4502'8092—dc22
[B]   209004751

ISBN-13: 978-1-4165-9910-4
ISBN-10:   1-4165-9910-X

B
SPE

To Liam and Stella—
Fate made me a parent.
Your amazingly beautiful souls made me a mommy.

In loving memory of Mimi La Rue
1998–2008

Contents

MOMMYWOOD

Introduction

Near the end of my first pregnancy my husband, Dean, and I went to an appointment for an ultrasound. It was always exciting to see the fetus by ultrasound, but this time it would be a special, 3-D ultrasound—an amazing new(ish) technology that allows patients to see a clearer picture and doctors to bill insurance companies more. Instead of the usual staticky, hard-to-discern image, we'd be able to see exactly what our very own baby looked like floating in my belly. It felt like this was the moment when we'd be meeting our little miracle for the first time.

The doctor squeezed the self-warming goo on my belly and started moving the wand around. We already knew that the baby was a boy. Now the doctor was saying calming, nonspecific things like "Looks good . . . all good. There's his little foot . . ." Actually, who am I kidding? I have no idea what the doctor was saying. For all I know he said, "You're having six babies and you'll be delivering them through your ear," because something had me distracted. I was focused on the screen, staring hard at my baby's delicate face. There he was, all perfect. Head, eyes, ears, but, well . . . I didn't want to admit it, even to myself, but something was bothering me. His nose. I kept coming back to it. I was worried, well, it's just that . . . it looked a little—was I even allowed to think this?—it looked a little, um, large.

As soon as the thought entered my mind, I tried to shut it down. I kept trying to look at the rest of the baby. Skinny little legs . . . nose. Teeny tiny hands . . . nose. Heart—a little heart that you could already see beating! One of the most incredible sights anyone could ever witness—*nose!*

Maybe this was one of the many facts about fetuses I'd skimmed over in all those having-a-baby books I'd bought and really, really intended to read by now: you know, "Babies can look blue at birth." "Their eyes are puffy." "The umbilical cord resolves itself." I racked my brain: was there anything I'd read about ultrasounds making noses look exaggerated? Or noses being out of proportion at birth? Yeah, yeah, wasn't there something about that?

At last I couldn't help myself any longer. I pointed at the screen and asked the doctor, "Is that true to life?" He replied with something overly scientific about the way the sound waves are reconstructed and the surface and the internal blah blah blah. Not very helpful. Inside my head I was screaming, *Oh my God, does he have a huge nose? Just tell me!* but I was having trouble asking it directly. I knew it was wrong to care, but I did. So I tried to put it as delicately as I could: "Does his nose look . . . normal?" The doctor nodded. "Of course, of course," he muttered. Hmm. That still wasn't really satisfying. I timidly ventured, "You don't think it's a little big on his face?" Glancing up at the screen he said, "It's possible he's pushed up against the placenta. That could distort or exaggerate the features." Okay, now we were getting somewhere. I said, "So it's a normal-sized nose?" The doctor reassured me that my baby would come into the world with a nose that was ready and able to breathe. You know how doctors can be. They assume "normal" means "healthy"—so respectable, so nonsuperficial, so not what I was looking for. "Healthy" was good news, very good news, the best news. But not exactly what I was worrying about right then.

On the way to the car Dean was quiet. Once we had gotten in and were driving, he finally said, "I can't believe what I just witnessed." Uh-oh. Dean sounded angry. He went on, "We were looking at a beautiful, healthy boy—our baby!—and you're worrying about the size of his nose?" Well, of course the baby's health was what mattered the most! I worried about that every day. But this was the super special 3-D ultrasound, the one where we saw our baby moving in three-dimensional space. Once all vital signs looked good, wasn't I allowed to want a cute baby? I told Dean, "I couldn't help it. I said what I was thinking. It came into my head, and I wanted to know. Should I have just sat there wondering in silence?" Dean sputtered, "Are you really that shallow?"

Suddenly it hit me. I was picking apart my unborn baby. I couldn't help but flash back to the day my mother told me I'd be pretty "as soon as you have a nose job." I always claimed, only half joking, that that moment had scarred me for life. And now here I was worrying about the facial features of my *own* child, before he even had a chance to breathe air. At least my mother had the decency to wait until I was twelve to start in on me. Was I a hypocrite? Was I destined to replicate the mistakes my mother had made?

Mothers are supposed to think that their children are gorgeous no matter what. What if I didn't? What if I'd inherited some mutated gene from my mother that caused us to feel nothing but disappointment in our offspring? Oh my God, did I have the Joan Crawford gene? It made sense: whenever I saw moms showing off little-old-men babies—you know the kind: wrinkled, puffy, and world-weary—much as I love babies, part of me always thought, *Can you not see that you've got a mini Ed Asner on your hands?*

As soon as we got home I called my friend Jenny. Jenny was pregnant with her second baby and I knew she'd be honest with me. I told Jenny what had happened at the doctor's office. She said, "Are you kidding? I do the same thing. That's what girls do." Jenny said that once we feel reasonably sure that the fetus is healthy, we assess the features of all family members, immediate and distant, and assemble them into a vision of the ideal genetic descendant. Then we watch closely to see how the baby's features line up against that vision. "It's totally normal."

I was a little relieved. I might be shallow, but at least I had company. Later, when Shane, Jenny's second child, was born, she'd be the one to say, "Come on over, but he's no looker." (Let the record show that Shane is now a gorgeous child and of course Jenny thinks so too.)

Talking to Jenny made me feel better. But then I started wondering. Is that what *all* mothers do? Or is it what *we* do—Jenny, me, and all the equally shallow friends around us? Are we normal moms, or are we living in Mommywood?

As anyone who read my first book or has glanced at the tabloids in the last couple decades knows, I didn't have a normal childhood. My dad, Aaron Spelling, was an extremely wealthy TV mogul. I starred in *90210*—a show that my father produced—for ten years starting when I was sixteen. My mother and I have a difficult (at times publicly so) relationship—when we have a relationship at all. My whole childhood I wished I had a normal family. I've spent much of my adult life working to prove that I'm a real person, a normal person, not the punch line of a joke.

Now I have two children of my own and I want them to have a normal childhood. I want them to have a happy life. I want to have a close, loving, joyful relationship with them for the rest of my life (though I realize that the teenage years are a bitch). My mother and I had and have our troubles, but I was raised by a nanny I called Nanny, and I learned plenty about being a good mother from her. Now is the time for me to take what I learned and to be the mother I always wished I had. But knowing you want to do things differently doesn't mean you know how to escape the way you were raised. This wasn't just about me worrying about the size of my unborn child's nose. Now I was struggling with the much greater fear that when push came to baby, I was going to be just like my mother.

I grew up in the public eye. I don't think of that as a bad thing, but I think it's pretty obvious that being regularly watched, photographed, written about, and sometimes chased like an escaped prisoner by the paparazzi must have had an effect on me. It's made me care a little too much about how I and, by extension, my family, look in pictures, be they candids, glossy magazine shots, or—ahem—ultrasound images. Obviously that's something I have to work on. But what else is there? What other special effects has my unusual upbringing had on me?

How has Hollywood shaped me? How will it shape my children? Can a celebrity be a good mother? Can children grow up in the spotlight without being scarred for life? Will my children play kickball in the street with the neighborhood kids, or will they grow up thinking that the reality show cameramen who follow us around are their best friends? Can I give my children privacy from the media but still let them have friends and neighbors like normal kids? Above all, will my children and I develop the relationship that I had always dreamed of having with my own mother? I may care about a nose for five minutes in a doctor's office, but these are the real issues that I worry about every day. I want my children to have a happy, normal childhood, but "normal" can be pretty elusive around here.

The fact that my life isn't normal doesn't make it any less real. My struggle to balance work and home life may show up on TV sets across the nation, but lots of moms who aren't on TV have the same challenges. My attempts to get along with my neighbors may be complicated by their preconceived notions of who I am, but I'm still a mother, hoping her children can be friends with the kids next door. I grew up in great wealth, but I work as hard as the next person to make a home, to pay for school, and to give my children a world of choices and opportunities. I strive every day to be a good mom, like moms everywhere.

Hollywood is a glittering, glamorous, superficial land of dreamers, wannabes, and stars. Mommywood takes place on the same set—the palm trees and eternal sunshine of Los Angeles. But casting is difficult and requires nine months of faithful commitment to rocky road ice cream, plus labor and delivery. The lead roles are played by stars who are finicky, in need of nonstop coddling, and around two feet tall. My own Mommywood life is full of drama (an awkward encounter with a former costar at a children's birthday party), tragedy (the death of a diva pug), horror (when poo meets pool), and farce (being the only one in costume at a Halloween party), but at the center of it is the greatest love story I've ever experienced, greater than any love story on the small or silver screen, the same amazing love story that all mothers go through with their children.

This is the story of my definitely amateur, sometimes serious, often bumbling, never-to-be-finished attempt to make it in . . . Mommywood.

Life in the Fishbowl

If a parent's job is to present the world to their children, then I had to think hard about how the choices I made for my life were affecting my son, Liam. If anyone's upbringing defined a Hollywood childhood, it was mine. Now Dean and I had a reality show, which meant our lives were a spectator sport: even our son's birth was part of the ongoing series. Like me, Liam was literally born into a world of television.

Granted, there were some differences between our childhoods from the very beginning. Liam didn't live in a mansion with a butler or a driver. His mother wasn't wearing diamonds the size of a chestnut to do her two-finger daily inspection of the maids' dusting thoroughness, and nobody was joking about renaming a network after me and Dean the way they called ABC "Aaron's Broadcasting Company." Every night my father left his TV shows on the studio lot, whereas when we're shooting *Tori & Dean* there are cameras in our house and following us around. There were no paparazzi trailing us when I was growing up, and even if there had been, they would have been stuck way down my parents' driveway at the gate. Now not only are paparazzi cameras clustered outside our house almost constantly, but when Liam flips through magazines in doctors' offices he says, "Mama? Mama?" as he turns the pages. Doesn't matter if it's *Us Weekly, Time,* or *Highlights*. He expects to find a picture of me in every issue.

This will sound a little crazy, but (actually, save me a little space and just assume lots of the details of my life are prefaced with the phrase, "This will sound a little crazy, but . . .") Liam actually prefers the weeklies to the cute board books and picture books we buy for him. I guess there's something that Britney and Angelina deliver that Babar and Horton just don't do for him. If I'm preparing Liam's breakfast and he gets quiet, I look up to check on him. More often than not I find him sitting on the floor, turning the pages of a *People* or *Us Weekly* magazine that he's grabbed from the table. Some days our baby nurse, Patsy, and I take the kids on a walk to the nearby Coffee Bean. We stop at the corner newsstand to pick up the new weeklies (yes, I'm addicted). I buy Liam, now twenty months old, a no-sugar-added, coffee-free, chocolate iced blended and an English scone. Then he sits in a chair, drinking his iced blended and looking at magazines like a big boy. If big boys are fascinated by who wore what to the Oscars.

One night Patsy had some family over—about five women—

and was making them dinner. Liam was excited when they arrived. I saw that he wanted to show them his favorite toys, maybe his room, so I said, "Monkey, show them your house." (Monkey is what Dean and I call Liam because he danced and bounced like a little monkey in his Exersaucer.) So Liam ran to the living room, his favorite room, and grabbed a weekly that was sitting on the table. He waved the magazine in the air, crowing, "Oooh, ooh, Mama." I was a little embarrassed, but I figured they probably didn't get exactly what he was saying. Chances were they just thought it was odd that a baby was proudly showing them a magazine.

Then one of the women said to Liam, "Are *you* in the magazine? Is there a picture of you?" Liam got an excited look on his face, made some of those hyperventilating-like grunts toddlers make when they've been understood, and flipped through the glossy pages until he found the inevitable photo. It was him and me. He pointed with his chubby finger and said, "Mama, Mama!" He was exceedingly proud. It was his big moment. The woman asked, "Where are you? Are you in the picture?" Liam beamed and pointed to himself next to me. Then his face got really serious. He turned the pages intently, looking, looking, until he got to a certain page and stopped. He pointed to a picture, smiled broadly, and said, "Dada. Dada!" We all looked down. It wasn't a photo of Dean. Liam was pointing at a picture of Patrick Dempsey. Boy, did the women love that. They were all like, "Is your dad McDreamy? What a scoop!"

It's not just that Liam thinks family photos arrive in glossy magazines with the Friday mail. He's also completely obsessed with the paparazzi. When he sees them he screams in delight and smiles for the cameras. There's no trying to block them by holding him inside a jacket or pulling up a stroller blanket to create a shield. Even when he was only one year old he seemed to know exactly what I was trying to do—ruin his shot!—and would get mad.

One time I was shopping in a store and a swarm of paparazzi appeared from out of nowhere. Maybe I'd stepped on one of their nests or something. There must have been fifteen of them with huge cameras lined up to snap pictures through the store window. This happens sometimes. I normally suck in my stomach, try to remember not to pull my underwear out of my ass, and otherwise pretend they're not there. But Liam doesn't exactly have the same instinct. His round tummy is cute and he knows it, his diaper is usually firmly in place, and he hasn't quite grasped the concept of pretending. This time I looked away from Liam for one moment, and when I looked back I saw that he was standing face-out in the window display, staring at the crowd of photographers. They were all going crazy, taking picture after picture of him, and he was totally mesmerized by the flashes of light. I couldn't resist pulling out my own (much smaller) camera to take a picture. In it you see Liam from the back and (I have to admit) a rather pretty meteor shower of flashes in the window behind him.

Cameras have surrounded Liam since the day he was born. They're both mundane and fascinating to him the way lamps or doorknobs are mundane and fascinating to other babies. When we moved into our first house, a tech company came to install top-of-the-line baby monitors that let you watch the baby on video online. Why such fancy monitors? Well, because we got them for free on condition that we let the company film the installation. Such is the world of celebrity perks: it's not all handbags and high heels. So the tech company had their film crew in the house, with cameras and lights. When Liam saw them he got so excited you'd think it was Christmas morning. At first I thought, *Oh look at my son, the budding filmmaker. He's excited because he thinks they're lining up a great shot.* Then I realized that he thought the cameramen were *our* cameramen. We'd been on hiatus for a month, and he thought the crew for our show had returned. You could see it on his face. He was thinking, *They're back! Everyone's here! Finally, my family's all together again!*

Okay, so that's a little weird. My kid expects to be surrounded by cameras. But (thanks to another celebrity perk) he also is accustomed to remote control toilets. And if my husband worked for a dry cleaner maybe Liam would expect his T-shirts to be lightly starched. Or if I were I hairdresser he'd request a trim every other day. Lots of people have jobs that affect their children in one way or another. As far as these things go, I don't think we're inflicting major trauma. Thanks to the reality show he's very socialized. He's not scared of people. Or large cameras. Or electronics. Or sudden flashes of light. Take this kid into an alien spaceship and he'll feel right at home.

I don't worry about the cameras per se. The part of leading a public life that I worry about the most is something I can't really change and that's this: people know who Liam is. People on the street in our neighborhood. People who see us when we travel. People we run into on vacation. Liam will grow up being recognized, and as his parent I have to think about how it affects him.

This hit me recently when Dean and I went on a tour of a preschool for Liam. We were in a classroom watching five cute little kids in a yoga class. (Pause for laughter. So Los Angeles. We're all hippie health nuts. Okay, resume playing.) As those kids worked on their downward-facing dog poses, I looked around the classroom and noticed little cubbyholes with names on them. The name "Deacon" jumped out at me. How did I know that name? Then I realized, *Oh, that's the name of Reese Witherspoon's son. Deacon.* Looking back at the kids, I saw that, indeed, one of them was Deacon Phillippe. I recognized him. How weird is that—to be able to identify a four-year-old? He's not a celebrity, and I don't have any personal relationship with him or his parents beyond occasionally being on the same page of magazine photos showing that we celebrities are just like you, but I recognized him in his preschool yoga class. I thought, *This is going to be Liam's life.* He'll forever be recognized because of who his parents are. It could have been worse. We could have named him Blanket. (Just kidding. Blanket— it's a lovely name.)

The truth is that Liam's life is already like that. We were

walking into a department store and a mom looked at him and asked, "Was he in my son's class?" Then "Is he a catalogue baby like my daughter?" Then she recognized me, said, "Oh, never mind," and hurried away, embarrassed. The same thing has happened to me ever since I can remember. People come up to me and say, "Didn't we go to high school together?" I'm thinking, *Um, only if you went to the fictional school appearing in* Beverly Hills 90210.

I've actually always found it kind of sweet that when people recognize you from magazines or TV, they think you're an old friend, that you go back a long way together. It's like we all shared something, even if we were on different sides of the experience. But when I saw and recognized Deacon, for a moment it was like I was outside the fishbowl looking in. I was like those fans, like any mom anywhere recognizing Deacon or Liam, and I felt a little sad. These young kids are already being seen in a different way, and they have no say in it. Does it make their lives harder? Does it change the way people treat them? Does it change the way they see the world? I wish I knew the answers.

I grew up in Hollywood, but like I said, I didn't grow up with the paparazzi—not like there are now. At each event there was maybe one photographer, a legitimate professional whose job was to capture the event, like a photographer at a wedding. Now there are masses of people with cars and cameras stalking celebrities, shooting up your skirt as you climb out of a car and bombarding you as you enter or exit an event or restaurant.

The pictures of me with my parents at events show that I was shy but used to that single flashbulb. Liam would think it was strange if we came out of a restaurant and there weren't four or five photographers with flashes going off in his face. This is the first generation of kids growing up with that.

In the outside world, like any mom, there's only so much I can do to protect my child. I shielded his baby carrier, but he's too old for that now. I'm not going to lock him away. I'm not going to put a mask on him. I don't want him to feel embarrassed about or restricted by who he is. There's a point at which the protecting can do more harm than the threat itself.

I can control the reality show—the cameras inside my house that expose Liam to millions of viewers every week. It's my choice as a parent to allow that to happen. But I love doing our show. I actually think it's changed the way people see us. Some of the people who recognize me on the street now treat me more like a friend than a celebrity. A couple will tell us that they had the same fight that Dean and I had, or a mom will tell me she has the same issue with her son that I've had with Liam. It actually makes me feel more normal. The media puts celebrities up on a pedestal; even when they say we're "just like you," one page later they're separating us again. The show is my chance to say that even though our world may be a little odd, we're still just people. I hope Liam will be proud to have been part of it one day. The show is my livelihood, and it allows me and Dean to spend more time with Liam. It keeps our family together.

I didn't choose my upbringing, but now I'm making decisions about my own children's lives and that upbringing is the only personal experience I have. I skipped college to stay on *90210*. I worked on *90210* for a total of ten years—so long that when I finally walked out into the bright sunlight of the real world I couldn't imagine being anything other than an actor. I still can't. I have no other life skills. Entertainment is my life. I was born in it. I grew up in it. I'm stuck in it. And I love it. I can wonder about taking Liam out of the spotlight until the end of time, but the truth is I don't really feel like I could support my family any other way.

I glanced back at the yoga kids, now rolling on their backs in happy baby pose. Deacon seemed fine. The other kids in his class didn't see him as different. They were all only three or four. School, I hope, will be a safety zone for Liam, where he can be himself without all the cameras.

When Liam is older, I'll try to give him options. I mean, I'm a proud mother and I have to say that I think Liam's a natural-born entertainer. He is funny and outgoing and loves to be the center of attention. But I'm going to make sure he has the college education I missed and the self-confidence I lacked. I want him to feel free to pursue whatever life appeals to him. When it matters to him, I hope I'll have given him all the tools he needs to be able to live out of the spotlight if that's what he chooses.

Baby Honeymoon

When Liam was born, Dean and I took two months off *Tori & Dean: Inn Love*. We had a maternity/paternity leave. It was a brief, idyllic period when Liam got to be a baby just like any other baby and I felt just like every other mom.

At first I was breastfeeding constantly. But I wasn't producing enough milk, so I supplemented with a bottle. We fell quickly into a rhythm. Liam would sleep, wake up, nurse, have a bottle, play, go back to sleep. He slept a lot, and I had downtime during the day for the first time in years. Patsy (remember, our baby nurse) got me back on soap operas. I hadn't seen soap operas in years. But nothing changes on soap operas. They practically move in real time. Here were all the same characters and story lines that I remembered from ten years before. In one day I was completely caught up. And hooked. So the schedule was more like watch *All My Children*, nurse Liam, watch *One*

Life to Live, give Liam his bottle, watch *General Hospital,* nurse Liam, watch *Oprah,* and so on. It was a taste of what being a stay-at-home mom would be like, and I loved it. (Okay, a stay-at-home mom with full-time help—not realistic, I know.)

After a little bit we started to take Liam out in the world. I'd never had a baby before. I didn't know what to expect. But Liam was happy to go anywhere. We'd bring him to a restaurant in his car seat carrier. If he was awake, he'd look around and smile. If he was tired, he'd take a nap. Having a baby was a piece of cake. Patsy told us not every baby was so accommodating. We'd been blessed with an easy baby and we took full advantage. We were blissfully happy and we wanted to celebrate. We went out for brunches, dinners, and drinks. It was the hotel hop—the Four Seasons for cocktails, the Peninsula for tea, the Beverly Hills Hotel for early dinner. Sometimes it was just the three of us: Dean, Liam, and me. Sometimes we brought Patsy to show her places she'd never been before and tell her stories about what had gone down at one hotel or another in my single days. Every day we went out to walk and eat at least one meal with Liam. The baby nurse, the fancy hotels, the time off, the easy baby—these made us different from some, but the feelings we had were just like those of any new parents. It was so exciting. We were so proud.

When our two-month break was over, we went back home to our duties running our bed-and-breakfast, and our cameras followed for the second season of *Tori & Dean: Inn Love.* We packed up our car, drove up to the inn, showed Liam around, and settled in. Within a few days the phone rang. It was an offer from the TV station that was launching the first season of our show in England. They wanted us to come to London to promote the premiere. I ran to tell Dean the news. Dean's initial reaction was to say, "No way! We just got geared up to work here. Liam is two months old. We can't do it."

I said, "But they'll fly the whole family! And Patsy! To Europe! We should do it. It'd be really great. The show could follow us there and film the trip."

Dean still thought the idea was insane. He said, "Okay, it's crazy to do this right now. We're still adjusting to the new baby. But as long as we're there, I want to take you to Scotland." Dean's family is Scottish. He wanted me to see the homeland. So now we were going to London and Scotland. And then to Toronto to do press for the Canadian release of the show. Our little trip grew to three weeks long.

We boarded the flight and walked to our seats in first class. Peter Falk had the seat in front of me, and as soon as he saw that we were traveling with an infant, he pushed the call button. We heard him grumbling and talking with the flight attendant, and then they moved him upstairs (it was one of those double-decker planes with two stories of first-class seats). We were a little insulted. Why wouldn't someone want to sit near a baby? We didn't know it was unusual that Liam never fussed. Now I don't blame Peter Falk for moving. How could he have known that Monkey was an angel baby?

Liam did everything with us. He slept in cribs at the hotels.

He came to every stop we made on our media tour. We went on *Friday Night with Jonathan Ross,* who's like the Jay Leno of Europe, and Liam and Patsy hung out in the green room waiting for us. The chef Gordon Ramsay was on the show the same night we were. Dean is a huge fan of his. Gordon got us reservations at his newest restaurant, Maze. It is one of those hot, trendy restaurants that you usually need to book far in advance. We brought Monkey in his pajamas. As we ate the chef's tasting menu at nine p.m. on a Friday night, Liam was snuggled up in his car seat, sound asleep. That was the moment when I thought, *Wow, you don't have to change your life for the children.* Liam was fine. More than that, he was happy to be with us.

Part of me worried about the Peter Falk factor—that people would judge us for bringing a baby to a fancy restaurant. There was something awkward about arriving at a hip, upscale restaurant and asking them to put the stroller somewhere. It felt a little inappropriate. But we knew Liam would be quiet and we figured a little extra gear never hurt anyone.

In Scotland we took the opportunity to visit some local bed-and-breakfasts, just to see the difference. They were all very cute and charming. One day I didn't feel so hot and I wondered out loud if I could be pregnant again. Once the idea entered my head, I liked the sound of it. Dean and I knew we wanted more kids. Monkey was only two months old and I was still naïve about how children would affect our lives. Being a parent seemed so easy. And I'd loved being pregnant so much. I missed being pregnant. I thought, *Great, perfect, another one.* I felt a little sad when I found out I wasn't pregnant. Maybe it was soap opera withdrawal, with a touch of jet lag. But I knew it would have been crazy: we weren't ready yet.

As we flew home with our peaceful babe in arms, I thought about how much had already happened in Liam's short life. If this was what raising a child and being a TV star meant, then so far it seemed harmless. Not just harmless, it was great! Liam was traveling. He was seeing the world. One day we'd take him back to Maze. We'd tell him how young he'd been when he first went. When we returned, he'd be old enough to taste the pressed marinated foie gras with Lincolnshire smoked eel, baked potato foam, and dill, or the confit rare-breed Sussex pork belly, pig's head, quince confiture, and parsnips. He'd see the land of Dean's ancestors again, and next time he'd remember what he saw. It wasn't a "normal" childhood, but we could make it a good one.

It was still probably too soon to tell, but having Liam didn't feel like a disruption. It felt like a gift. When work started up again, my soap opera habit was gone for good. No more midday TV. No more working on Liam's baby book. My days of being a stay-at-home mom had been all too brief. What I most regretted was the state of the blanket I was knitting for Liam. I started the blanket on the set of *Smallville* in Vancouver, just after we'd announced that I was pregnant. I fantasized that he would take it to college and say, "My mom made this for me before I was born." Then, when he got married, he'd show his wife the blanket and say, "My mom made this for me before I was born." One day he'd have his own little boy. He'd give him the blanket and say . . . Oh, you get my point. When work kicked in again, I had to put the blanket aside. It's in a storage bin somewhere, still unfinished. If I stayed home to complete it, we'd never be able to afford for him to take it away to college. But I figure I still have time to work on it. I have until he's old enough to leave for college, don't I?

Daddy's Boy

Leaving Liam to work on our show was an issue for me. Of all the things I wanted to do differently from my own mother, most important was that I wanted to be there. I always planned to raise my kids myself instead of leaving it all to a nanny. But I'm a working mom. I have to have help when we're doing the show. There are even some days when Liam's babysitter is with him all day long. It's really hard for me. It's an ongoing struggle, and it's one I expected. What I didn't expect was the challenge of being married to a hands-on dad.

Ever since Dean and I met, we have spent all our time together. Then we started spending all our free time in a threesome. Um, I'm talking about Liam, of course. Dean loves children, and that's part of what attracted me to him. Liam has a poopy diaper? Dean is on it. Liam takes a tumble? Dean's there before he hits the ground. Time to get Liam out of the car seat?

Dean's already doing it. I want to do all those things for Liam, it's just that Dean always gets there first. When it comes to parenting he consistently beats me to the punch. He swoops right in there so fast that I'm left saying, "Um . . . I can do that . . ." to a no-longer-crying baby or an empty car.

When we brought Liam home from the hospital, the first thing Dean said to our baby nurse, Patsy, was "I change a mean diaper." Within minutes they were having a showdown, demonstrating their flawless high-speed diaper changes and swaddling techniques. Meanwhile, I was still in the beginner's ring. I was like, "Excuse me, guys? The cartoon characters go in the front, right?"

There's a reason he could change a mean diaper: he'd done it before. Dean has a son, Jack, from his first marriage. Dean's experience often comes in handy. Back when I was pregnant, I'd gotten excited about a cool high-tech diaper pail and Dean said, "Oh, Jack had that one. It doesn't work." Later, when Liam had blisters on his toes and it turned out to be hand, foot, and mouth disease or hoof, tail, and tooth disease or whatever, Dean just said, "Jack had that, it's no big deal." Even when Liam had a seizure (more on that later), Dean was unfazed: "Jack had those too. He grew out of them." He saw Jack learn to walk; he heard Jack learn to talk. It's great that Dean has experience. It's nice that he's calm when I'm worried. But even though we share all of the big parenting moments, bad or good, I don't get to share the newness with anyone. It makes me sad sometimes.

From the very beginning, whenever Liam woke up, Dean flew out of bed, grabbed the bottle, and went in to him. That was great, but it happened every morning, and I started to feel like I never had a chance to give my son his bottle. As far as Dean was concerned, it was no big deal. He heard the baby, grabbed the bottle, and went in. But in my mind, who would be the first to get to Liam became a race. I started calculating: if I have the monitor on my side of the bed and make myself wake up early enough, then I'll see his head pop up before he makes a noise and I can flip off the monitor and shoot out of bed before Dean stirs.

I know how ridiculous this complaining sounds: "Husbands, they're always trying to do more than their share of the child rearing. Are you with me, mommies?" But it affected me because of how I was raised and how much I'd told myself that *I* was going to be there for my child at all times. Plus, Liam was getting older. He was changing from a blob (albeit a lovable one) into a baby who could express desires. As soon as he could speak, he started turning into a Daddy's boy. When Dean walked into the room, Liam screamed, "Dada!" Meanwhile I walked in and . . . I could be the plumber. Not even—a plumber at least has cool tools. If we were in the car and Dean got out to pump gas or get a coffee, Liam got hysterical, even though I was sitting right there saying, "It's okay, Liam. Mama's here. Dada will be right back." It bugged me. The doctors always said, "Oh, kids go back and forth. Today it's the dad. Tomorrow it's the mom." My friends said the same thing. It was a phase. But for Liam, today was the dad, tomorrow was the dad, the next day was the dad . . . When was it going to switch to me? In the back of my mind I couldn't help wondering if there was something he wasn't getting from me. Maybe he wasn't feeling the maternal connection. Maybe I was repeating the past.

There were times when I was holding Liam and he'd scream and cry and lunge for Dean. I know this happens all the time: a baby wants his father. But when Liam gave the smallest sign that he wanted to be with Dean, I'd think I'd already failed. I'd hand him over, saying, "He hates me. My own child hates me." I even had a moment when I decided that there was a maternal scent. You know how dogs can smell if people are dog people? Well, maybe there was a smell that babies recognized as coming from a maternal person and *I didn't have the smell.* Or worse— maybe I had an antibaby smell! Maybe it ran in the family. Maybe it was the Candy Curse! I was so afraid of becoming her that I convinced myself I wasn't meant to be a mom.

Finally, Dean sat me down for an intervention. He said, "You have to stop saying Liam hates you. Ever heard of a self-fulfilling prophecy? You're a really good mom. You just have to believe in yourself."

You don't start believing in yourself because someone tells you that you should. You have to make changes. Maybe it was a phase, but even so I needed to spend more time with Liam—more *alone* time. I know I'm lucky to have a husband like Dean, but when you have such an enthusiastic partner you kinda forget how to function solo.

One day it came time for Liam's swim class and Dean couldn't go with me. This was my chance. Operation Make Liam a Mama's Boy had begun. I was excited to get some time to myself with my son, and I could feel reasonably confident that he wouldn't lunge for Daddy's arms when Daddy wasn't anywhere in sight. But as I plunked him awkwardly into the car seat and fumbled with the straps I realized, *Wow, I don't actually take him in the car by myself very often.* I was always with Liam, but how much of the heavy lifting did I actually do? Dean made everything look so easy. I felt like a new mom all over again.

Liam's swim teacher doesn't work at a regular indoor pool with a locker room. She has wealthy clients who let her use their saltwater pools all day for lessons. Their properties (in Brentwood and Beverly Hills) are so large they probably don't even notice she's there. Once I got Liam out of the car and safely in the pool, I thought we were golden. Liam is a crazy-good swimmer. He's, like, the next Michael Phelps. He just wants to spend all of his time in the water. So in spite of my prepool bumbling, he was having a great time, splashing and kicking and practicing blowing bubbles. Then his swim teacher said, "Oh, he pooped," and handed him to me. Yipes. I was the mom. Naturally I'd change his diaper. I'd changed his diaper a million times by now (sorry, landfills). Except this was a *swim* diaper. And it was full of poo.

Either you know this already or it's too much information, but swim diapers aren't rigged quite the same way as normal dia-

pers. Swim diapers have a tough job. They have to keep in whatever comes out. Without them, babies would put the "poo" in
"pool." So they don't have convenient Velcro openings. You can't
just untape, wipe, and be done with it. Instead, they're like little
pants. The load is kind of trapped in there. Good news for the
other swimmers, but once I had Liam in my arms, I had no idea
how to get that swim diaper off while adequately containing its
contents. That is to say, I feared the poop.

I must have looked as helpless as I felt because the teacher
shouted over, "Some people do it over the trash can." All the
other moms who were there with their kids glanced over at me.
The pressure was on. Now I was supposed to suspend Liam
over the trash can with one hand while stripping him down
with the other. Huh? Was that supposed to help me? How
many hands did she think I had? I couldn't get a visual on the
midair strip-down, so I went back to basics. I laid Liam down
on his towel. I pulled off the swim diaper. Again, either you
know this already or it's too much information, but when poo
is exposed to that environment (pool water, a sopping swim
diaper, a hyper child—the trifecta), it loses its structural integ-
rity. There was no . . . cohesion. Just crumbles of poo everywhere. A horror show.

I went in for the kill, but a few swipes later I was out of wipes
and still facing a seemingly insurmountable mess. I swear, there
was actually more there than when I'd started. Liam writhed
and struggled to break free from my less-than-sure grasp so he
could get back in his beloved pool. With the heroic sacrifice of

his swim towel I managed to get him clean(ish), but when I was done, my operating table looked like a colonoscopy gone very, very wrong. I rolled up the diaper, the uncontained poo crumbles, the wipes, his bathing suit (he could finish the lesson in his clean swim diaper), and all other contaminated items and potentially contaminated items into his swim towel, picked it up—and stopped. Yes, there was a garbage can right there, but I could imagine what the other swimmers would be saying if they saw me throw away a poo-smeared towel. *She can't change a diaper and she throws away towels as if they grow on trees.* The garbage can was not going to happen. I stuffed the whole thing into my diaper bag. I'd deal with it at home.

I may not be the most graceful mom in the world, but grace isn't the point. I don't have to be a perfect mom. I can be bad at changing swim diapers or clumsy at stroller-to-car transfers. I just want to be there. To laugh with Liam. To watch him grow. To make sure he knows how loved he is every step of the way. I was a Daddy's girl, and I always wonder how that affected my relationship with my mother. Liam might be Daddy's boy for the rest of his life. There was no way I was going to let that— or a little poop—stop me from building my own relationship with him.

Later that afternoon Dean came across the towel bundle in the hallway. He pulled back a corner and wrinkled his nose. "What have we here?" Oh. That. Yeah, Dean had a good laugh over that one.

Is She or Isn't She?

When Liam was born I was happy. We were showing him off and celebrating at hotel restaurants across Beverly Hills. Having a baby didn't make me want to diet. It made me want to indulge. And breastfeeding made me hungry. I knew I had some baby weight to lose, but I didn't want to think about that right away. Some celebrities may be making life hard for other moms by showing up in magazines two weeks after giving birth looking like they've never had a bite of ice cream, much less carried a baby, but I'm not one of those people. But being in shape is part of my job. Every mom wants her old body back, but usually the harshest critic is the mom herself, looking in the mirror at the pants that used to fit but now have soft belly (sounds nicer than it looks) bulging out over the top. The weeklies are my mirrors. I knew that if I didn't get to work and lose the weight, I'd be hearing about it from them, and they'd be much tougher than I'd be on myself. I dieted and exercised three times a week until eventually, when Liam was six months old, I hit my goal weight.

Now you may think that I was excited to hit my goal weight because it meant that I was healthy and fit. Nuh-uh. Because now I looked great? Nope. Because the weeklies wouldn't have a field day? A little. But the real reason I was so excited to get back to this weight was that now I could shop. I love to shop, and—let's face it—maternity clothes don't count. There are some very cute ones out there, but you're still making the most of a limited selection. Now I was back in the real world of clothes, clothes, clothes! I was so excited to shop again. I went to Fred Segal and splurged on a pair of skinny jeans. Okay, the truth is I splurged on four pairs of skinny jeans in all different washes. I was bad. It was wrong. Dean was shocked. You wonder why I went into debt after so many years on *90210*? Fred Segal is on the list of reasons. But I was just nuts about those skinny jeans.

When I stopped breastfeeding Liam, my ob-gyn, Dr. J, put me on the pill, but I didn't like the side effects, so he phoned in another prescription. I'd never heard of this pill, so I read all the accompanying information carefully. Mistake. There was such a long list of side effects, I got paranoid. What if I got an aneurysm? Or breast cancer? I'd already taken the first pill, but the second night I was so nervous that I didn't take it. That evening Dean and I had sex. Right afterward I said, "Baby, I didn't take that pill today." I know, maybe that information would have been useful to convey *before* the sex. But Dean just said, "Oh, it's fine, it's fine."

I flashed back to a phone call I'd gotten just a week earlier from my friend Jenny. Jenny, whose son Shane is two months older than Liam, had also had a bad experience with a new birth control pill. She'd stopped taking it. She and her husband, Norm, had had sex one time, and she'd said, "Norm, I think I'm ovulating." She called to tell me that she was pregnant with her third.

Suddenly I felt like I was starring in the Lifetime movie presentation of *My Phone Call with Jenny*. Just like Jenny I had gone off the pill. Just like Jenny I'd had sex once. Now, just like Jenny I went to the bathroom and said, "Babe, I think I'm ovulating." I didn't say, "Norm, I think I'm ovulating." That would have been weird. "Watch," I told Dean, "I'm sure I just got pregnant." After that night I stayed off the pill, but we took precautions. Still, I knew how that phone call with Jenny had ended.

Soon after the night in question I made an appearance with the Pussycat Dolls at their show in Vegas. I came out wearing a sequined black strapless dress that hit me above the knee. It had Velcro up the side, and after a few minutes I ripped it off to reveal an outfit rivaling Britney Spears's outfit at the VMAs in ambition, but I don't think I risked the same response. I'd known this night was coming and had been working hard. Two weeks earlier I hadn't been sure I'd reach my goal, but in those last two weeks it was as if my body was like, "Okay, okay, I don't want to embarrass you." Everything tightened up. I introduced the different performers, doing little monologues and jokes. At the end I posed with the Pussycat Dolls and they said, "We hear Tori can do a trick on the pole," so I went over and did a spin. I felt really good standing up there with my newly flat tummy. It was my big "back in shape" reveal.

A month later I felt a little crampy and decided I really should take a pregnancy test. I had one left over from when I was trying to get pregnant with Liam. I took one of those tests where one pink line means you're not pregnant and two pink lines means you're pregnant. There was one line, definitely. And then there was a hint of a shadow of a second line. I showed it to Dean. He said, "No, you're reading it wrong. That's not a line." Clearly I needed more tests. Lots more.

I didn't want to be seen (or, God forbid, photographed by the paparazzi) purchasing pregnancy tests, so I dragged my best friend, Mehran, to the drugstore with me. He and I have been best friends since high school, and every time Dean goes out of town, Mehran and I have a sleepover, staying up late to watch horror movies and eat piña colada Yoplait yogurt. When Dean does guy stuff, like scuba diving or motorcycle racing, Mehran is there to fill in. We go get pedicures and go shopping. Mehran was the natural recruit.

I stood on the other side of the store, in the first-aid aisle, while Mehran picked out a pregnancy test. I pretended to be contemplating my wart removal options, though, come to think of it, being outed as a warthog would be much less flattering than being outed as possibly pregnant.

After what seemed like hours Mehran came back across the store with a pregnancy test. It said it was ninety-eight percent reliable. We could do better than that. I sent him back to try again. But the design of the next pregnancy test looked cheesy. I wanted more scientific-looking packaging. Back Mehran went. Finally we settled on a test with high reliability and an acceptable design. There were no ambiguous pink lines on this test. It would say "pregnant" or "not pregnant." Nobody was going to accuse me of reading *that* test wrong.

We headed back to my house and I drank lots of water and peed on all three sticks. Mehran and I waited a few short minutes for the results to appear. Was I pregnant? The first test said "pregnant." The second one said "definitely pregnant." The third one said, "Ask again later—nah, just kidding. You're totally knocked up."

Jenny and I would be pregnant together for the second time. Some women who live or work together get their periods at the same time. Apparently Jenny and I get pregnant at the same time. I'd had all of a week to live it up at my goal weight. Now I was four weeks pregnant. I looked down at my Fred Segal skinny jeans and sighed. I knew they weren't long for that body. I'd just given away all my maternity clothes. I mean, I knew I was going to want at least one more child, but I thought we'd wait till Liam was a year old to start trying, and by then all of my maternity clothes would have been out of style. As it happened, Liam was only seven months old (six when we conceived)! He wasn't content to hang out with us in his carrier anymore. He wanted to wiggle around, explore, eat solid food, and make a mess. I couldn't imagine what the workload was going to be like with two.

But I remembered how much I'd loved being pregnant. It calmed me. I felt safe and completely at ease. I loved the feeling that I was completely responsible for protecting and taking care of someone else. We were taking care of each other. I was never alone. Call it pregnancy hormones, but I'm convinced that pregnancy gave me the sense of connection that I was missing with my mother. I was caring for a child, but I didn't have the fear that I was doing it wrong.

Mehran, my gay husband, had guided me through the testing phase. Now it was time to tell husband number one. I was nervous about telling Dean. My heart was pounding just because it was big news: I didn't really think there was a chance he'd be anything but excited. There was no doubt that we wanted multiple children together. Things were just happening a little faster than we'd anticipated.

I put Liam in a blue shirt and taped a little sign that said "I'm a big brother" to the shirt. Then I called Dean up to the bedroom. Liam was in bed with me. I handed him to Dean. No reaction. "Babe," I said, "look at Liam's shirt." Dean sort of chuckled. Like the way you'd chuckle if you were pretending to get a joke but actually had no clue. Dean has many fine qualities, but I had to walk him through it: "What does the shirt say? . . . Right, and if Liam's a big brother, that means . . ." It took longer than Dean would like to admit, but suffice it to say that before the night was over he was made to understand that he was going to have another child.

Dean was psyched. He'd been psyched when I thought I was pregnant in Scotland, and he was happy now. I mean, neither Dean nor I had an extreme reaction to the news. It wasn't "Oh, shit!" or "Oh, yes!" We had always talked about wanting a boy and a girl. Of course any baby is a blessing, but we discussed how many boy babies we'd have before we'd stop trying for a girl. Dean had read about spinning sperm to try for the gender you want. A lot of people might look down on this, but we talked about whether we'd feel comfortable doing it. Was it messing with nature? Would it feel weird? We thought when Liam was a year and a half we'd talk to a doctor about what the research showed about spinning. Or we could see what the old wives' tales said about timing and positions. When I got pregnant without looking into any of the girl planning, I immediately thought, *Oh, okay, I guess I'm going to have a boy.* Dean had his son Jack from his first marriage. We had Liam. I just thought, *Dean shoots boys.* No part of me thought I would naturally have a girl.

Come January I was three months pregnant and we were ready to share our good news. But my life is not entirely my own. I lost the baby weight for my image, and now I had to keep my pregnancy under wraps for business reasons. My book *sTORI telling* was due to be published in March. My publicist said that if we announced or acknowledged my pregnancy beforehand, then all the magazines would run big pieces about me. If they ran big pieces about me now, then when the book came out they'd all say, "Oh, we just had Tori on our cover. We can't do that again." So my "team" decided that I had to do everything I could to hide my rapidly growing belly from the media until the book came out. By then I'd be five months pregnant!

Luckily, right before I got pregnant, a company in New York called Porter showed me a beautiful black cashmere coat. It was heavy and thick and hit me just above the knee. They said they wanted to give it to me. I didn't think I'd ever have a chance to wear a cashmere coat in Los Angeles, but it was chilly in New York on that trip and the coat was so gorgeous. Long story short, I did not turn it down. Thank God it was fall and thank God for that coat. When my belly needed hiding, which was almost instantly, the cashmere coat became my personal paparazzi shield. When I put it on, my blossoming pregnancy disappeared. Now you see it, now you don't. There were heat waves that fall, but no matter how hot it got or what the occasion, I was wearing that same cashmere coat.

I loved being pregnant, but I hated hiding it (especially when it meant feeling like a walking furnace). The longer I waited, the more I wanted to tell people. I wanted to wear a tank top, have my belly show, and be proud. I wanted to share my good news. It was joyful. Hiding it made me feel like my life was not my own. But as the magazines began to speculate about whether I was pregnant ("Is she or isn't she?"), keeping it a secret started to be about more than timing the announce-

ment for the book. It was about my privacy. I started to feel
that choosing how, where, and when the news came out was
the way to make my life my own again.

So little in my life is private. The press quickly reveals
whatever we don't disclose in the reality show. The pregnancy
became the one thing that I could hold on to and have for just
me, Dean, and the close friends we told. I wanted to tell people
when I wanted to tell them, instead of having *Access Hollywood*
suspect and confirm it. Why should they or any other news
magazine get to choose when and how to announce something
so intimate? It was so weird to have those magazines calling to
say, "Can you just confirm your pregnancy so we can tell everyone already?" Um, no!

"Come on, lady. It was ninety degrees yesterday and you
were wearing a friggin' cashmere coat." Sorry, no!

As the book's publication date approached, my cute little
belly was not so cute and little anymore. The buttons on my
beloved cashmere coat were starting to pop. I sent photos of
my belly to my publicists with an email saying, "I don't think
we can hide this anymore!" Finally, my "team" agreed that I
would confirm my pregnancy on the cover of *People* magazine,
and there would be a book excerpt in the same issue. I was
five and a half months pregnant. It was about time. I'd lost the
baby weight for the weeklies. I'd hidden the pregnancy from
the media. Now, no more contortions. I had a reprieve to be a
pregnant mom, as is.

Round Two, Round Again

My pregnancy was public, and public fodder. Being pregnant on TV was a little hard at first. I was on a reality show, which sometimes meant that when I came downstairs in the morning, I'd walk right into a scene. I came from a background in scripted TV, where not only do they work on your hair and makeup for hours, but they carefully light every single scene and pick flattering angles so everybody looks perfect. There are no real surprises in a scripted show. On our show I often had no makeup on, and I'm far from a professional hairstylist. I just had to accept that I couldn't predict what was going to happen and that I was going to look like crap at times.

Hair and makeup aside, sometimes I felt absolutely gigantic. When I was getting my ultrasound—talk about unflattering!—I had at least three chins. Seriously. I think my neck was carrying a baby too. I was horrified when I saw myself on the footage. But I got over it pretty quickly. I figured, if I'm going to show the real me, people won't expect me to look perfect. In a scripted show if you don't look good, that's a legitimate problem, a violation of the viewer's expectation. But everybody knows that people don't look perfect in real life. Maybe it's even a good message—a nice contrast to the perfectly lit, professionally styled actors you see on scripted shows. At any rate, I got used to this new standard pretty quickly, and after that it was a relief to feel like I didn't have to look like some TV-manipulated version of myself. I could just be.

My attitude wasn't always this casual. During my first pregnancy I worried about what might happen to my body. In Mommywood, every mother's obligation is to make herself look as hot as possible through all stages of being pregnant and raising babies. I went into my first pregnancy worried about stretch marks. But then I discovered fabulous belly creams! I became obsessed with belly creams and slathered them on every day. I figured if I used them, I'd be fine, and I was. Phew.

Also with Liam, I wasn't prepared for losing sight of my lower region. Nobody tells you that's going to happen. I'd say, "Dean, how's it looking down there? Do I need to shave?" But of course I couldn't shave. So Dean had to shave me. He'd hold up a mirror and say, "See? How'd I do?" Or he'd take a picture with his BlackBerry to show me. Definitely never thought that would happen. It brought my then-new husband and me to a new level of intimacy—one that we figured was good preparation for childbirth.

Now, for the second pregnancy, I knew what to expect. I thought I'd be a little savvier when it came to the stretch marks. I did a little research. It turns out that there is no scientific evidence that belly creams work. They don't really do anything. If you look closely, some of them even say that they reduce the "appearance" of stretch marks. So they're, like, cover-up? So much for the belly creams. Ridiculous. I'd like to say I said "Screw it" and dumped the belly creams. But, oh, that Internet. It had more to say. The web told me that stretch marks are hereditary. Uh-oh. My mom had stretch marks! The fact I hadn't gotten them the first time didn't mean I was in the clear.

The web was telling me that there was nothing I could do to ward off permanent stretch marks. I had to just wait and see. I was feeling more relaxed about my pregnant body, but that didn't mean I was ready to adopt a wait-and-see attitude when it came to having permanent red lines wiggling along my hips. So I made an executive/superstitious decision that there had to be a reason for the belly creams. They couldn't just exist because someone was capitalizing on the vanity of pregnant women, could they? Oh, what the hell—I decided to use them anyway.

I lined up six different jars of belly cream on my bathroom shelf. Each one made different claims and had different compelling ingredients: shea butter, lavender, avocado, grapefruit seed extracts, marshmallow root. Gotu Kola extract, Vegolatum, TriLASTIN. Every night I'd dip into each one of them, one after the other, and ritualistically rub the cream into my belly. I must have smelled like a New Age salad bar. But I couldn't give up a single cream, because what if there was only one that really did work? There was no way of knowing which one it might be, and I wasn't taking any chances. Yes, I told Dean, women are full of contradictions. Being seen with triple chins on national television: no problem. Permanent stretch marks: unacceptable.

Sometimes Dean would try to help with the elaborate belly cream ritual. He'd do a nice, calming application, taking his time, dipping into each jar, but he never quite got it right. He'd take too long or apply too thin a layer. I'd say, "That was great, thanks," and then as soon as he walked out of the bathroom, I'd dip, dip, dip, and slather it on. Now, it happens that I didn't end up with any stretch marks, after either pregnancy, but I doubt it had anything to do with the belly creams. Nonetheless, I am pleased to report that I had the softest belly ever. Those belly creams—we should slather them all over our entire bodies every day. My pregnant belly was like butter. (I vowed to maintain it, but of course once the baby was born I never slathered again.)

I felt so much more comfortable being pregnant the second time around that I was willing to take pictures—in my bikini. I agreed to do a poolside pregnant-in-bikini photo shoot that appeared in *Life & Style* magazine. After that photo shoot was published, magazines kept asking me why I did it. "What made you decide to pose in your bikini?" or "Did you struggle over that bikini photo shoot?" I heard those questions time after time. I started to notice that it was only the female interviewers who asked about the bikini photos. The male interviewers never asked about them or about my weight. For whatever reason, the women were much more interested in the "body" story.

The truth is that I didn't think twice about it at the time. I love the way women look when they're pregnant. I thought I looked good. I especially loved my boobs. Pregnant boobs are the best, although I couldn't help wishing I had them with a flat belly. The point is, I felt great and I was happy. Why shouldn't I want pictures taken?

One person was particularly vocal about the pregnant bikini shots. It was—to my surprise—the stand-up comedienne and late-night host Chelsea Handler. I met Chelsea when I was working on my show *So NoTORIous.* My writers said they knew the perfect person to play my best friend, Janey, so I went to see her stand-up act. I thought she was hysterical. She came in to read for Janey, and we liked her. I supported her when we brought her to the network, but it didn't work out. Still, I thought she was totally cool, and I thought of us as friends. Not call-each-other-on-the-phone friends, but, you know, people who had met a few times and felt friendly toward each other. In other words, "best friends," in Hollywood lingo.

When I heard Chelsea had her own show, I was psyched for her, so I made a point to watch it. The first night I turned it on, there she was, blasting me. She doesn't just hate me. She obsessively hates me. I'm a running joke on her show. When the bikini shots came out she said on the air, "So I promised I wasn't going to slam Tori Spelling anymore because we have the same publisher, but I just can't help myself." She held up the magazine, opened to photos of me. "We just don't want to see this." Here I thought I was sending a positive message to women that being pregnant is beautiful and we should be proud of our bodies. Of course, Chelsea had an important message too: after comparing a person to Seabiscuit for a while, you should shift and say she looks bad pregnant, just to keep it fresh. Got that, everyone?

On one hand, I guess she's using me as the butt of her jokes because she knows the public is interested. That means I'm noteworthy. Or infamous. I'm used to that. On the other hand, I really did think we were friends. I don't know what's more Hollywood—that she's busting on a friendly acquaintance for cheap laughs, or that I thought we were actually friends in the first place. Producers from *Chelsea Lately* actually called a couple of times to ask if I would be on the show. Why would I be on the show when she's so mean to me? Maybe that's the most Hollywood aspect of it all—that I would come on a show after being treated like that, no hard feelings, because it's just entertainment. It's not real. And besides, I'm supposed to want the exposure that being on the show of someone who hates me would generate.

Even at home my pregnancy wasn't my own to enjoy or suffer. Both my real husband and my gay husband claim to have gained baby weight when I was pregnant. The first time—with Liam—Dean ate whatever I ate just to keep me company. If I was craving McDonald's, he ran out to get McDonald's for both of us. If I wanted dip made from a packet of Lipton's onion soup with Ruffles potato chips, Dean wanted onion dip with Ruffles. Mehran, my gay husband, took this reaction to another extreme. When I was four months pregnant, Dean went to Canada to visit Jack. Mehran was staying with me, as he always did. I woke up at three in the morning to discover that Mehran's side of the bed was empty. I went downstairs to investigate and found him alone in the dark kitchen, wreaking havoc on a bag of Doritos. He had a midnight craving. Mehran claims that as soon as I was pregnant, he was absolutely ravenous for nine months.

Pregnancy is the world's greatest excuse for decadent consumption. During my first pregnancy I went crazy with the food. Brownie bites, old-fashioned glazed doughnuts, microwave mac and cheese—you name it. But then I found my true craving. Dean fixed me a bowl of rocky road ice cream. Aha! After that Dean fixed me a bowl every single night. I'd always been skinny, so I didn't worry about how much I was gaining. I was sure it would come right off after I had the baby. But it hadn't been as easy as I thought it would be. There was way too much exercise and not-drinking-wine for my taste. If possible, I didn't want to go through that again. So during the second pregnancy I was trying to be more mindful of what I was eating. I mean, I still wanted carbs all day long, but I tried not to eat so terribly.

Then, two months into the pregnancy, Dean asked, "Aren't you craving rocky road?" Well, now that he mentioned it, I was. Thanks a lot. I told Dean not to buy the ice cream, but the next day he brought it home anyway. Surprise! He started bringing me a generous bowl every night. I had to eat it: I didn't want to hurt his feelings.

That was bad enough. Then one morning, Dean asked, "What do you want for breakfast?" and while I was thinking it over, he said it. Those fatal words. "How about some rocky road?" The world stopped. It's like my eyes were opened for the first time. Rocky road for breakfast! Of course! Whoever said one bowl a day was the limit? It never would have occurred to me, but here was the man I loved, suggesting it as if it were a perfectly reasonable way to start the day. Who could say no to that?

Minutes later there I was, happily spooning ice cream into my mouth. I looked over at Dean. He was enjoying the same breakfast. Out of solidarity. Before long Dean was offering me rocky road ice cream for breakfast, lunch, and dinner. My thoughtful husband. Then suddenly it dawned on me. Dean always fixed two bowls of ice cream. He ate it every time I did. This wasn't a sacrifice out of solidarity. *Dean* was the one who wanted rocky road back in our lives. *Dean* was the one who wanted ice cream for breakfast! This was all his fault! And yet I knew *I'd* get blamed for it after the baby was born. Both Dean and Mehran complain about the weight they gained during my pregnancies. Dean says, "I'm still trying to lose the twenty-five pounds of baby weight." Mehran likes to observe, "I gained more with the second." And here I thought the pregnancy was one thing I could call my own.

The Family Curse

Now remember, Dean and I were sure I was pregnant with another baby boy. Dean had already fathered two boys. But also during season two of *Tori & Dean,* before I was pregnant, I'd brought Dean to visit Mama Lola, the voodoo high priestess who once cleansed me from a curse. Mama Lola said, "You're going to have more babies." Liam was only four months old. I said, "How many do you see?" She said, "Three." Dean and I smiled at each other. That was what we had been thinking. Then I said, "I'd love to have a girl." Mama Lola looked down at the cards and studied them for a moment. When she looked up she said, "Well, you want a girl but what if you have all boys?" That seemed to settle it. Baby number two would be a boy.

As far back as I can remember, I've always wanted to have a baby girl, but my relationship with my mother—have I mentioned my mother yet?—was so fraught that I couldn't help feeling nervous about how I would do with a daughter. To some extent all parents act and react according to how they were reared. Some people might model their parenting on what their parents did. I wanted to model my parenting on something more abstract—what my parents *didn't* do. But maybe having a girl was too close to home. What if I brought all my confusion and trouble with my mother to the relationship? I'd rather not have a girl at all than be a bad mother to a daughter. So when I found out Liam was going to be a boy, I thought, *Okay, maybe that's what's meant to be. Maybe I'm meant to have all boys.* I got comfortable with that idea, and I started to like it.

At one of my regular checkups, Dr. J said it was too soon to officially call it, but he thought I was having a girl. Dean and I were shocked. What? Impossible. We said, "No, no, no. It's a boy."

Dr. J said, "I would go on record saying I'm ninety percent sure it's a girl." After that there was a seed of hope, but neither Dean nor I really believed that it could be a girl. Later, at twenty weeks, we went to a different doctor for the quadruple screen sonogram. This time we knew we were going to find out the gender. As the nurse was doing the preliminary exam, Dean said, "Do you see what I see?" I did. We both saw a penis between the legs. When the doctor came in, he said, "What do you guys think you're having?" (He must do this to torture all his patients. What fun. For him.)

I said, "We think it's a boy."

The doctor said, "Really? Why do you think it's a boy?"

Dean pointed at the ultrasound and said, "That's a penis right there!" The doctor explained to us that we were looking at the labia of our baby girl, but we still didn't believe him. He practically had to pull his degrees down off the wall to convince us. Even when we had a detailed ultrasound again later in the pregnancy, we asked, "Are you sure it's a girl? Is that stuff between the legs still girl stuff?"

Okay, so Mama Lola doesn't have a perfect track record. Voodoo's an imperfect science. At the doctor's appointment when we found out that I was pregnant with a girl, I was so shocked and overjoyed that I completely forgot to worry about the size of her nose or any other superficial concerns. A daughter! I'd longed for a daughter for so long, but I never really thought I'd actually have one. My—our—own little girl.

In the car on the way home I started to think about the relationship I wanted with her. I would strike the perfect balance between mom and friend. I would never judge her. I would always tell her she was beautiful. I would give her all the emotional strength I could, the confidence and optimism to do whatever she wanted to do. The list I went through was all the things I felt I hadn't gotten from—you guessed it—my own mother.

As the pregnancy went on I started to get scared. Nothing was more important to me than to be a good mom. What if I was even more disastrous than my mom had been with a girl? What if all my hopes and intentions backfired and the past repeated itself tenfold? What if with a girl I became my mother all over again? What if I *was* cursed? Liam was so daddy-focused. What if the girl was the same way? What if both kids loved their daddy more and there was nothing we could do to change that? What if Dean was just a person kids love more than kids love me? Would I feel excluded? Would I pull away to protect myself? Is that what had happened with my mother—I was so attached to my father that she resented it? Then I remembered my first wedding and thought, no, she created our dynamic.

I don't want to go on at length about my relationship with my mom, but I want to explain how intense and destructive our dynamic was. It's a formative part of who I am and what I want to avoid as a mother. My pop-psych theory is that my mom couldn't stand the idea that I might have more in life than she did. At my first wedding she said, "I didn't have a big wedding. My parents couldn't afford it." When I told her how happy I was with Dean, that I'd found my soul mate, she congratulated me, but in the same email she gave me notice that she and my dad were selling the condo that I was renting from them right out from under me. After my father passed away, she said things like "I never had friends. Your father wouldn't let me." It seemed like something was missing from her life and she blamed me.

The way this dynamic played out was subtle but ongoing. Even when I was in my early twenties, instead of bonding we were competing. Beanie Babies—those little stuffed animals filled with "beans" instead of stuffing—were a big fad. They became collectors' items, with people trading them on eBay for exorbitant amounts of money, depending on how rare they were (or how rare people thought they might one day become). A few years later everyone suddenly realized at once that they were worthless, and the market crashed. They were like the tech stocks of the mid-nineties, except that everyone knew they were beans and fluff from the start. But during their peak, my mom and I got obsessed and started buying Beanie Babies on eBay. I'd bring my laptop to my dressing room at *90210* and be intently bidding on one animal or another. When my five-minute warning to be on set came, I'd be furiously clicking to add five dollars to my bid. Then I'd hurry out to stage cheering, "I just won the crab!" I had books cataloguing the world of Beanie Babies—how many of each were manufactured, what colors they came in, what they were worth. I received the Beanie Babies newsletter once a month and was a member of Beanie Babies of America. Eventually my business manager included my Beanie Babies in my monthly report. Under assets.

My mother was doing the same thing. She'd send me an email saying, "So, I was just wondering whether you've gotten Slither yet." I'd say no, and she'd respond, "Oh, I just got mine. I won it on eBay." I'd go online and see that Slither the Snake was going for $2,500. Some of the Beanie Babies were only released to small stores in certain areas. Once I found the coveted Princess the Bear, a special release for the Diana of Wales Memorial Fund, at a small store in New York where nobody thought to check. When I wrote to tell the big news to my mother, she responded, "Oh that's great. I have five." My mom's Beanie Babies were all tagged, numbered, and carefully sealed by her staff. I had piles and piles of Beanie Babies filling my apartment. Was collecting Beanie Babies a shared interest that my mom and I enjoyed pursuing together? It didn't feel like it. It felt much more like a competition. And I have a thousand worthless Beanie Babies in Ziploc bags in storage somewhere to show for it.

I imagine that in some way my mother thought we were bonding over the Beanie Babies. But again, it felt like she couldn't stand the idea that I would ever have more than she did. My mother may have loved me, but although she was able to give me things that she had missed—whether they were emotional or material—I think she felt angry at letting me have them. Was it because her mom hadn't made her feel good about herself, so she didn't want me to feel good about myself? If she didn't get to have a doting mother, why should I? That was my greatest fear. I hadn't had a doting mother; what if I passed the same resentment on to my daughter?

As my pregnancy progressed, Dean and I had long talks about my genuine fear of having a girl. I always told Dean that I felt like my dad had a hand in creating the competitiveness, the jealousy between me and my mom from an early age. He had doted on my mother, but when I was born he turned his attention to me. I worried about this with Dean. He's always dreamt of having a little girl. And I'm Dean's world. Were we set up for disaster? Even with both of us doting on Liam, I still felt like his focus was all Tori, Tori, Tori, but what if he stopped showing me that affection? I hoped that I would just be glad to see my children being loved, but what if something came out in me that I couldn't predict or control?

I made Dean swear to protect us all from this dynamic. When our girl came he had to make sure to love us both. He was like, "Of course, I would never love you any less." I knew that's what he would say, but it helped to hear it. I think it's important to talk about these tensions in any family. I saw an interview that Heidi Klum and Seal did on *Oprah*. Seal said that his priorities were in this order: wife, children, career. That made me stop and think. My first instinct was *Wait, kids don't come first?* Then I realized that in a way he was right. People have children and they're so dependent (and cute!) that the focus naturally turns to them. Children need more protection. They need more care. But you can't sacrifice your relationship as a couple.

I worried about our family dynamics, and I also worried about the caregivers. I was raised by Nanny, an amazing woman who gave me the foundation for how I want to parent. Without Nanny I wouldn't be the person I am today. But from my earliest fantasies about being a mother, I was certain that I'd never have a nanny for my children. Then we hired a baby nurse for Liam. We had to: we were going back to work full-time, and even if he was always nearby, we needed to make sure there was someone to hold him, to give him his bottle, and to put him down for naps when he was ready. We found Patsy, who felt like part of our family, but I still hoped I wasn't setting myself up for failure from the get-go by having someone come in to help me raise my child.

What I needed to keep reminding myself was that my situation was very different from my mother's. I didn't really have an option. I had to work in order to support my family. The same was true for this baby: I knew I'd be returning to work less than a week after she was born! If I didn't have a baby nurse, what would I do? I wasn't afraid of my children or reluctant to spend time with them; I was working out of necessity. I had help because I had to earn money. Of course, my mom was busy too. She had lots of Madame Alexander dolls (which I was never allowed to touch) to collect, label, and display "for me." Wow, now I *do* sound bitter.

What I have to come to grips with is that there isn't one perfect way to raise a child. Maybe our bond is closer when we spend more time together, but it doesn't disappear when I work. It's not the time, it's not the caregivers, it's not one interaction on one day. It's everything put together. Those hours and days, those choices we make as parents, little and big, they all add up. My goal is to make them add up to the strongest relationship possible.

What was my ideal relationship? I hadn't lived it, so I had to think it through. I started by reflecting on what, specifically, from my childhood I wanted to change for Liam, but especially for my unborn daughter. I decided to write down rules for myself, so if having a girl ever made me lose my grip on reality, I had somewhere to turn.

Here are the guidelines I created:

1. *The Madame Alexander Rule:* Getting your daughter a present and telling her she can't touch it (like my mother did every year with those ridiculous Madame Alexander dolls) is worse than not getting her anything. So I'll never get her anything. No, just kidding. I'll always get my daughter presents she can play with.

2. *The Bonwit Teller Rule:* Along the same lines as above, I'm not going to dress my daughter in clothes she doesn't want to wear. Especially not anything pastel. I don't know why my mother always made me dress up like a doll—especially when she had all of my dolls to play with. But as long as my daughter's clothing choices are within a range of acceptability, she can wear whatever she wants. Even (oh God, I can barely say it without gagging) pastel.

3. *The Rapunzel Rule:* If she wants shoulder-length—or ass-length, or floor-length—hair, she can have it. All I wanted growing up was long hair, and my mother made me get that same stupid bob for twelve solid years. (Are you picking up any sort of theme to these guidelines? Not that I'm bitter. Stupid bob.)

4. *The Nanny Rule:* Dean or I will always be there at night when she's sick or scared, instead of relying on a nanny to sleep by her side. I know that seems like an obvious one, but I just had to say it.

5. *The Ed McMahon Rule:* I'll let her invite whomever she wants to her wedding(s), and I won't invite celebrities I barely know just because they happen to be on the invitation list of someone I want to impress. (Unless it's Kate Winslet or someone like that. Then all bets are off.)

6. *The I-Paid-for-This-Wedding-and-All-of-Your-Furniture Rule:* Gifts I give to my daughter will never come with strings attached. Or ropes. Or intricate pulley systems that require the recipient to dance the cha-cha while wearing lederhosen.

7. *The Lonely Rich Kid Rule:* I'll let her go over to friends' for sleepovers. Even if I turn out to have as many crazy fears and paranoias as my father did (and I'm well on my way), I won't indulge them. I'll let her do what other kids do.

8. *The You-Must-Pay-the-Rent Rule:* If I ever buy a residence for her (as my mother did for me), I won't make her pay rent; at the very least, I won't raise said rent every year by having my money manager send my own daughter a notification by email. And to answer your question, yes, that happened.

9. *The Face-to-Face Rule:* You know what? Let's give this its own place: I'll never, ever communicate with my daughter through a money manager.

10. *The No-Such-Thing-as-a-Coincidence Rule:* I'll never show up at her wedding rehearsal dinner dressed like her older twin.

11. *The Parental Sponsorship Rule:* I won't offer to host a postwedding brunch, or any other party for that matter, and pull out funding the week before.

12. I'm looking at Rule 7: Okay, Rule 12 is that if I hear that there are gonna be boys at this sleepover, then forget it. She's staying home. And I'm disappointed that she didn't tell me about the boys. Wow, I'm already worried about this.

13. *The Beanie Baby Rule:* I won't pretend to bond while subconsciously competing with my daughter over who has the better Beanie Baby collection (or whatever worthless, short-lived fad it'll be in the future).

14. *The Champagne BMW Rule:* I don't know if/when I'll buy her a car, but I'm not my mom: if she wants the cheaper Volkswagen instead of the luxury car that I think complements her skin, she can have it. I'll use the savings to hire a private investigator to find out who the hell that boy was at the sleepover.

15. *The sTORI telling Rule:* If my daughter ever writes a tell-all book about me, I promise to take it as constructive criticism, to get us into therapy together, and not to retaliate by writing my own book.

16. *The Rule That Should Be True for All Mothers:* I'll love my daughter unconditionally, no matter who she is, what she does, or how difficult our relationship is.

On the other hand, I do have some fond memories from my childhood. And there were some rules I didn't disagree with entirely.

1. I wasn't allowed to go to summer camp. I see the draw—the lakes full of leeches, the rustic plumbing facilities, the insipid color wars—but I'm not sure I'll be able to let her leave me for so long at such a tender age.

2. Like me, she won't be allowed to make out with twenty-five-year-old chefs. Or any other household employees. Or anyone more than one year older than she is. Actually, I don't see why she has to make out with anyone, at all, ever. But I'm open to negotiation—after she's twenty-one.

3. Maybe it was inappropriate for my mother to watch *Invasion of the Body Snatchers* with me when I was only four years old, but if my daughter starts later, I wouldn't mind if she eventually comes to love horror movies like my mom and me.

4. I might secretly hide beautiful seashells for her to find on the beach, just like my mom did for me. I'm not opposed to deceit if it's with the purpose of nurturing wonder and

joy. After all, isn't that the whole philosophy behind Santa Claus? But I'll make sure that she doesn't find out the truth the same way I did: reading it in *OK!* magazine.

5. Those big theme birthday parties that my mother threw for me? Oh, they're in my blood now. Monkey, ladybug, rodeo, zoo, fairy, Santa in the tropics . . . I've got big dreams.

Monkey Business

I have some idea of what kids' birthday parties are supposed to look like. Balloons tied to the front door. Pin the tail on the donkey. Maybe a hired magician or clown. Some sheet cake from the local grocery store. Done. I have that picture in my head, but I'm not sure where I got it. My childhood birthdays were completely over-the-top Hollywood. There was always a custom cake from Hansen's, the legendary Los Angeles bakery. There was always a moon bounce and there were always live animals—be it a poodle performance or Smidget the miniature horse. There were at times any number of the following: Ronald McDonald, a Michael Jackson impersonator, a children's fashion show. Growing up I remember going to a swimming party at Diana Ross's house for her daughter Tracy, and to a party for Cheryl Ladd's daughter, Jordan, on a big lawn at her grandfather's house. I can't say I have any memories of simple, homespun birthday parties.

When Liam's first birthday rolled around, my honest-to-God intention was to have a small party for him. I would avoid the excesses of my parents. Our celebration would be small, rational, and appropriate. Plus, I was seven months pregnant. This was no time for a big, crazy blowout. I always thought that it was silly to have a birthday party for a one-year-old anyway. They don't remember it. You might as well just have a few friends over, hand the child a cupcake to smash, take a picture of said child with a party hat on and the cupcake smeared all over his face, and be done with it. But as soon as I got together with my gays to start planning, something happened to me. Some primal urge kicked in. I went into a fugue state. My eyes grew wide like David Banner's and I turned into a party-planning Hulk. There was no stopping me.

Dean and I have always called Liam "Monkey," so it was a no-brainer to have a monkey-themed party. My first stop was . . . Hansen's. I wanted a cake shaped like a monkey, but not just any cake. I met with the owner, who remembered the Raggedy Ann cake I once loved and looked forward to every year. Are you picturing an ordinary sheet cake decorated like Raggedy Ann? Please. This Raggedy Ann was sitting up. She was three-dimensional and covered with dabs of ruffled icing that gave the whole cake a kind of soft, textured look. That Raggedy Ann cake was one of my treasured memories. Yes, yes, it had to happen. I ordered the same cake for Liam, but in the form of a monkey holding a banana. With banana-flavored cake, of course.

Next, there had to be live animals. A live monkey was obvious, but how could we top it? Hmm . . . aha! *Two* live monkeys! Steve Martin's Working Wildlife was bringing Suzy the chimp, and then there was an organ-grinder monkey who would do a carnival-style song and dance. I thought the two monkeys could hang out, maybe pick each other's nits, but Suzy the chimp's managers were not thrilled to hear about the organ-grinder monkey. They said that Suzy and the organ-grinder monkey were not to cross paths under any circumstances. They required a fifteen-minute buffer between the two appearances. I'm sure there was a very good reason, but it came across a little Hollywood. Diva monkeys couldn't share the set with each other, *Desperate Housewives*–style.

I couldn't find a monkey-themed moon bounce, but I had read Liam a Curious George story where he goes up in a spaceship. I was hoping that would tie the moon bounce in thematically somewhere in the back of Liam's mind.

Once the basics (go ahead, mock me, I deserve it) were in place, I should have stopped. But (damn you, Internet) when I found out I could hire a little train to drive in circles around the party, well, I knew Liam would love that. And of course we needed lots and lots of food. People had to eat! Especially the pregnant hostess and her sympathetic husbands.

As I was planning, it became clear that there was no way this "little" birthday party would fit in our backyard. Our backyard was almost all swimming pool aside from a small grassy area. We needed a spacious lawn to accommodate the food stalls, the animals, the cake table, the moon bounce—not to mention the train! We needed a new location. I asked around, and a friend volunteered his parents' house. At least *someone's* grandmother was willing to provide space for Liam's first birthday party. Ahem.

Everything was planned and ready. The morning of the party Liam started cutting a molar. He was one. These things happen. Yet another good reason not to make a one-year-old's party into a mega-event. Poor Liam was miserable. The notion that we'd planned this whole spectacular day for (mostly) his benefit went whizzing right past him. He had no interest in Suzy, and even less in the organ-grinder monkey. He refused to ride in the train. The people who were transporting the moon bounce to the site of the party had car trouble. Then they got lost. The moon bounce didn't show up until halfway through the party. Then the time came for the cake. I was so excited. I had visions of Liam reaching out to touch the monkey, eyes wide with amazement. Maybe he would try to grab the monkey's cake-banana and wind up with a handful of delicious yellow icing. Ha, ha, funny pictures! But when we brought Liam over to the cake to sing "Happy Birthday" to him, he started screaming. He was terrified. The cake was bigger than he was. Liam pulled away, shielded his little eyes, and shrieked in terror as if he thought the giant cake-monkey was trying to kill him. Even far away, on the other side of the lawn, he wouldn't take a taste of the little morsel of cake that I tried to feed him. Hansen's cake? A total bust. But at least now he'd be able to say that he had a Hansen's cake from his first birthday on. The tradition had begun.

We had all this amazing little kid food. Mini pigs-in-a-blanket. Mini hamburgers. Mini corn dogs. Mini grilled cheese sandwiches. Banana mini milkshakes. Chicken nuggets. All Liam wanted was one of the bananas that we'd hung from the trees as decorations. A plain old, regular, non-made-out-of-Hansen's-cake-and-icing supermarket banana. That banana was the highlight of the party for Liam. He sat in his high chair and quietly enjoyed it. Oh, and he was a big fan of the Dippin' Dots. It reminded me that for all the lavish parties my parents threw me, the two special treats that stood out every birthday were McDonald's—each child got a Happy Meal bag—and the mind-blowing party trough that Baskin-Robbins used to deliver with scoops of all thirty-one flavors. I could have had anything my heart desired (if my mother desired it), but what I loved most were the same delicacies that almost any kid with any amount of money would enjoy.

I know Liam didn't have the time of his life and won't even remember the party. I know that, on some level, it was an excuse to gather my friends together. But looking around that day I felt like everyone who came was instrumental in our lives. They'd all known me throughout my pregnancy. They'd known Liam since he was born. His party may have been wasted on Liam, but it wasn't purely selfish. I hoped that Liam would grow up knowing that he was surrounded and celebrated and loved by our close friends and us. This was his family.

Here's what I learned from Liam's first party: I would have had an amazing time if it had been a smaller party, with just the close friends who know my day-to-day life. We invited one hundred people. It felt like an event, not my son's birthday party. I go to so many events and it's usually the same drill. Sometimes we'll take friends, like Bill and Scout, to an Emmy party or a similar event. Afterward they always say that it was so much fun. The buffet, the bar, great music, a couple of people they know. But for me, parties like that are always about doing business—schmoozing and talking to fans. Both are important, but they suck up all the time that I might have spent talking to friends, having a drink, or exploring the buffet. I never make it to the food. People stop me every inch of the way. Afterward someone will say, "Oh, there was great art in that space." I never see any of it. I get into a room and don't move forward. Once I went to an NBC/Universal event with NBC affiliates and press. I made it four feet into the room, stayed in that one spot an hour and a half, and then we left. I never made it past the door.

At Liam's party there weren't any businesspeople. It was all people we cared about. People who cared about Liam. But when I'm hosting people I don't see very often, I spend the whole party playing catch-up. I felt like I greeted people from beginning to end. Dozens of five-minute conversations with people and my child's birthday was over. I was pregnant, and at the end of it all I was exhausted. We went home and I had to go straight to bed. All I could think was, *Thank God Dean and I got married alone.*

Okay, here's what you should be thinking right now: *Wow, an elaborate party that ends up being more about her than her child? She is her mother!* Now wait a second, no need for insults. I get it. I see the similarities. But here's the difference, and it all comes back to this whole Mommywood desire I have to raise normal, healthy children despite the crazy, weird world we live in: Liam may not want Hansen's cake forever. He may not want theme parties. And as soon as it's clear that he wants something else—boom. It's over. I want him to grow up understanding that he's unique and important, and that means "his" days really are about him, his mother's wishes be damned.

I know it can be hard reconciling your fantasies of who your children will be with who they are. My friend Jenny, who lets her three-year-old daughter, Delilah, dress herself, says sometimes it's torture to see the adorable dresses hanging ignored in the closet. One time we met at a restaurant and Delilah was wearing a halter dress that was probably designed to be worn with a T-shirt underneath. Her little nipples were showing above the top of the dress. She was totally happy and comfortable. But what seemed to be rankling Jenny most were Delilah's shoes. "I mean, would you ever wear those shoes with that dress?" she said. It was really offending her sense of style. I was enjoying Jenny's obvious anguish, but she said, "Just you wait. It'll happen to you too, and when it does, it's heartbreaking."

I thought back on the prissy pastel Bonwit Teller dresses that my mother made me wear year after year. And that stupid bob cut she insisted the hairdresser give me. Who knows why I didn't or couldn't rebel, but if next year Liam doesn't want another big party and would rather sit in a sandbox with a plain old cupcake, I'll be fine with it. When Liam is old enough to express himself, I'll do everything I can to make sure I listen and give him the parties that he wants. And should I overdo it, I'll let him hang out in his high chair, munching a banana, if that's his preference. Of course I mean this for both my children. If someday in the not-too-distant future our baby girl walks out in a green dress with orange socks and blue shoes or, even worse, insists on a bob, I don't think I'll be heartbroken. I think the ten-year-old in me will take vicarious pleasure in my daughter's freedom. And then maybe the ten-year-old in me will go ask my mother what happened to all those Madame Alexander dolls she gave me every year but ultimately kept for herself.

Liam's first party was over. I morphed back from Event Planning Hulk into plain old Tori, took a look at the disassembled train and monkey poop around me, and asked, "What happened?" When the episode of *Tori & Dean* aired showing Liam's party, my publicist got an email addressed to me from PETA. Though they had no idea where we hired the monkeys or how they were cared for, they still chastised me about the inhumane use of live monkeys as birthday party entertainment. That explained Liam's lukewarm reaction. Obviously they got to him first.

Once all the guests cleared out, Liam got his zest back. Dean took him into the moon bounce and he had the best fifteen minutes of his life up to that point. I watched my two boys laughing and tumbling in circles and felt the baby somersaulting in my belly. For all the planning, that moment felt like the real birthday present—for all of us.

The Suburban Dream

Once Liam's birthday passed, Dean and I turned our attention to practical matters: real estate. I wanted our kids to grow up in a real neighborhood, a normal neighborhood—one with sidewalks, and neighbors with kids, and people borrowing cups of sugar. The house in that dream neighborhood was linked to my fantasy of being a stay-at-home mom, but as far as I could tell, the staying-at-home part wasn't going to happen any time soon.

The success of *Tori & Dean* was a welcome point of stability in our household. The timing of Liam's birth was such that I had a couple of months off work, but with the comfort of knowing that I had a job to return to. But this baby girl was due to be born when we were right in the middle of filming our third season, and she expressed no interest in waiting an extra few months. Assuming I was in good-enough health, I'd return to work the day after I got home from the hospital. In my fantasy world, I would put my career and my finances on ice and take a year off the minute the second baby was born, but the reality was that we were lucky to have work, and sadly, it couldn't be put on hold for our brand-new baby.

In Hollywood, if an actor doesn't work for any period of time, the casting directors forget about her. It doesn't matter why you're not working—because you can't bear the thought of playing another FBI agent, because you want to take time off for a trip around the world, or because nobody will hire you post–jail term. (No, none of these reasons apply to me, although a trip around the world sounds nice. Minus the plane rides.) The point is, as an actor, if you're off the job for a few months, that's it. You're over. Or so it seems. All actors have had dry spells and remember how stressful it is never to know if or when we'll work again. The same way an athlete worries about injuries, or a fund manager worries that his investments will go sour, or a Beanie Baby employee might worry that the fad will end. It's part of the job. Actors live in a semiconstant state of fear and anxiety that we'll never work again.

I wish I could afford to be a stay-at-home-mom. I fantasize about taking Liam to a Gymboree class or going to Mommy and Me groups with the new baby every single week instead of just when I can fit it in. I imagined us living in a new neighborhood where I could walk the two of them to the playground in a double stroller every morning, then push the baby in the swing while keeping one eye on Liam in the sandbox. My friend Jenny is a full-time mom. She and I would soon have two babies the same age. We were already having Friday night family dinners with the boys playing together at one family-friendly restaurant or another. Our dream was to raise families together, and now we were, but wouldn't it be nice to do it . . . more? Sometimes I look at Jenny's life and wish it were mine: if she's pulled in multiple directions, it's by her two, soon to be three, children. She takes her oldest, Delilah, to preschool, then she might take Shane (Liam's buddy) to gym class. After preschool Delilah goes to ballet, then Jenny's back home making dinner. When Norm gets home from work, they eat as a family. I know she's just as busy as I am, and I know she gets stressed out, but she's doing mom stuff. She has one job. She never has the work versus family conflict.

I'm constantly working. I work seven days a week. It's not just the TV show. I have fifty million different projects and obligations. My jewelry line. My children's clothing line. Meetings about a new website. Talk show appearances. Building Dean's and my production company. Developing new ideas for TV and movies. Even writing books! For better or worse, I have the kind of fame where my name is a brand. I know it sounds weird, but we treat "Tori Spelling" like a business. What do people think of me? Do they recognize my name? Do they trust Tori Spelling's taste? Even when we're not working on the series, my life is a never-ending meeting about building the Tori Spelling brand. Not every actor goes this route: I suppose I could do the reality show and leave it at that. But I can't. I'm telling you, it's the curse of the Hollywood actor. It's impossible to turn down opportunities. So then I think, *I'll work my ass off now, earn bundles of money, and then I can be home with my family one day.* But we all know how that will turn out. I'll work hard for fifteen years, finally earn enough money to be home, but by then my kids won't even want me around. My prime earning years are their prime growing years. It gives me grief and guilt every single day.

I have no idea how to do anything but act. I always have lots of ideas for businesses, and our show made me realize I could actually give them a try. I started by opening a bed-and-breakfast, but it wasn't for me. Then I toyed with starting a french fry business. Can't you see it? A chain of stores with reliably excellent fries and excellent toppings in food courts across the country? In reality I'm not going to spend all day working a deep fryer. It would frizz my hair. But I still think it's a good idea. And I still fantasize about opening a Mommy and Me store—a store with a play area for children and staff to supervise them while their mothers shop in peace—but that hasn't gotten off the ground. I could make my famous red velvet cake and hold bake sales on street corners. We could move to the country and Dean could work in construction. I'm sure a life coach/spiritual guide/high voodoo priestess could give us some other options, but for now I feel pretty stuck in the life I'm living. I think lots of people are like this. We're afraid of what we don't know. And I like my life. I'm grateful for it. I'm just conflicted.

I can't control work, but I try to create more time to be with my children. Like any mom (except my own), I have scaled back on the personal maintenance. The hair extensions? Gone. The pedicures? Infrequent. I'm single-handedly trying to bring back the closed-toe shoe, and it's not for fashion's sake. I'd love to get back in shape, but if I have an hour or two off, I don't want to spend it taking a yoga class or slogging away on the treadmill. I complain about my weight and Dean tells me I should go to the gym. But an hour-long class away from Liam? I can't do it. The only weight loss program I can manage is dieting. Being distracted by children during dinner is a great diet program; I don't have to go to the gym nearly as often! I discovered that I could get healthy the family way—by taking the kids out in the double jogger, by swimming or biking with Liam, by cooking nutritious food for the whole family. Rather than take time away from the family, I made our family time wholesome for all of us.

I wasn't going to be a stay-at-home mom, but at least Dean and I could find a home in a place that felt more like a neighborhood. When Liam was born we were back and forth between friends in L.A. and the bed-and-breakfast. Then we rented a house up in the canyons with no flat sidewalks where we could walk with the stroller and no real sense of neighborhood. I grew up in a house with a driveway that was so long I can't remember ever walking to the bottom of it. So now I fantasized about living in a real neighborhood, where we could go out for walks, chat with the neighbors, and maybe even make some friends with children the same age as ours! As my second pregnancy progressed, Dean and I decided to buy our first house. Maybe the suburban dream house would balance out my working mom angst.

We found a house on Leave It to Beaver Avenue (let's call it Beaver Avenue) in a part of L.A. called Westwood. The neighborhood was flat (yay!), with mostly two- and three-bedroom houses on nice but not huge plots of land. Anyone walking through it could immediately imagine that it was a pleasant neighborhood with lots of unpretentious people. It was a very real neighborhood—by L.A. standards, anyway. The houses were close together, not town houses but right up against one another. Most of them were one-story houses that had been in the same families for generations. The younger people on the block had grown up there and the houses had been passed to them from their parents. Our future house had a pool that filled most of the backyard and it had a patch of green grass where the dogs could do their business. When I looked at that backyard, two images filled my head: Liam swimming to his heart's content, and the amazing cocktail parties we could have.

The people who sold us the house told us what an exceptional neighborhood it was. Everyone was friendly and we were lucky to be moving in that spring, because every third year Beaver Avenue threw an incredible Fourth of July block party. That wasn't all. Every Halloween our neighbor had a wine bar for the adults and cupcakes for the kids. Another neighbor told me that a nearby block had a party—a "progressive dinner."

Five houses in the neighborhood would host. The first house would serve cocktails. The second house would serve hors d'oeuvres. The third house would serve appetizers. The fourth house would serve the main course, and the last house would serve dessert. The neighbor said, "We should do that on Beaver Avenue," and I was completely on board: "We should!"

As soon as we closed on the house, we started doing some minor work on it, and every time we came to check on the progress, there was some new neighborhood feature to be excited about. We saw kids playing out in the street: would their parents be our new best friends? There were people taking walks in the early evening: it must be so safe! I was going to have neighbors! A neighborhood! I got a double stroller and imagined that as soon as the baby was born I'd take long walks with the two babies. The double stroller was the übermom accessory. I was on my way to a minivan and proud of it. But life doesn't always go according to plan, and for all my fantasies, I was no June Cleaver.

People Randomly Die

I had a wonderful husband, an adorable son, and a daughter on the way. We had an income, and now we even had a family home that was almost ready for us. My dream life was coming together. But for all my ongoing efforts to be and prove myself a normal mom, I had to come to terms with the fact that—Mommywood aside—I'm just not one hundred percent sane. I've always had irrational fears. A sniper would open fire on me as I walked across a parking lot. The baby would kick a hole in my uterus. A shampoo bottle would get upset if it was facing the opposite way from all the other hair care products. And always, always, the plane would crash if I wasn't wearing a certain necklace or carrying a particular stuffed animal. Or both. Now that I was a mother, and very nearly a mother of two, I was supposed to be the grown-up. I was supposed to reassure Liam when he was frightened. I was supposed to be a point of calm in the storm. A rock. But here's the thing. In the past I always knew my fears were irrational. The way I kept them under control was by reminding myself how unlikely they were. But now that I was a mom, my irrational fears were replaced by a whole new set of worries. And these fears were real.

A week before our baby girl was born, Dean was out with Mehran getting a tattoo of all three kids' names. They were filming it for our show, although that little adventure didn't make it on the air. I was home with Paola, a babysitter we had hired as I reached the end of the pregnancy. I'd been having pain when I carried Liam, and my doctor told me I needed to stop lifting him up, so Paola came to the rescue. That afternoon, it looked like Liam was starting to get sick. He was running a fever, he threw up, and he was a little out of it. So we gave him a bath and some Tylenol and put him to bed. Then Dean texted me that he was going to be home in half an hour. It was 8:30. I told Paola she could go home, but she insisted on staying with me in case Liam woke up. (Remember? I couldn't lift him out of his crib.) I went to lie down in my room. Liam was in his room, next to mine, and Paola was downstairs watching TV with the video monitor. Next thing I knew Paola was sprinting upstairs. I came out of my room and asked what was wrong. She said, "I think he threw up," and hurried into his room. I followed behind.

When we found Liam he was blue and didn't seem to be breathing. His eyes were white, rolled back in his head. Paola took him into her arms, but he was limp. He wasn't moving or breathing. I thought he was dead. I froze in shock. Paola looked at me and said, "T, call nine-one-one." The phone was downstairs, and though I had lumbered slowly and painstakingly up and down those stairs throughout the pregnancy, this time I don't remember touching a single stair. I flew.

Paola brought Liam downstairs while I was on the phone screaming, "Help, help, I think my son is dead." The emergency operator was going through a greatest-hits list of emergency operator lines: "Ma'am, you have to calm down. Ma'am, just give me your information." I was hysterical as I somehow gave them my address and relayed their instructions to Paola. Thank God she hadn't gone home. All I could think was, *Oh my God, in a week I'm going to have my daughter, why is this happening? I was about to have my perfect family and now I was going to lose one child. Is this how it's going to be? Is one taking the place of the other?*

We laid Liam on his back as they instructed. He was still lifeless. Totally unresponsive. I wanted to wrap him in a blanket and run down the hill and meet the ambulance, but suddenly Liam's eyelids started to flutter. Okay, so he wasn't dead—that was really, really good—but I wasn't relieved yet. His eyes were still rolled back in his head. He still looked like he was dying. "Oh, hurry, hurry," I wailed into the phone.

Just as the EMTs came in—three minutes from when I called!—Liam gave a little cry. The guy on 911 said, "Oh, it's a baby!" They hadn't asked how old he was and I hadn't told them. The EMTs strapped various monitors to Liam's tiny chest and we all rode to the hospital.

Dean and Mehran rushed into the waiting room, where I was holding Liam. I was hugely pregnant, and so worried and exhausted. When I saw Dean's face I felt relieved. He'd take care of us. He'd make sure a doctor saw Liam. He'd take over from here. By then Liam's color was starting to return and he was whimpering, but he was still out of it. When he saw Dean, he reached out toward him. I handed Liam over. Dean, Liam's idol.

I was certain Liam had brain damage, but the doctors told me he'd had a febrile seizure, which is a convulsion brought on by a high fever. I'd never heard of it, but apparently what looks like death on a fifteen-month-old baby is actually fairly common and harmless. The seizure, which must have been what Paola saw on the monitor when she thought Liam was throwing up, takes everything out of the baby and he's totally zonked afterwards. Hence the unresponsive state. Later Paola told me she thought, *What happened to Monkey? He had a heart attack. He's dead.*

By the time we got home I'd gone through so much stress (and flying down the stairs!) that the baby—the other one— had dropped. She was on my pelvis. I couldn't move. I was screaming and crying with the pain. Dr. J said that we could do the cesarean three days early. Dean thought we should do it—he hated to see me in so much anguish—but I refused. I wanted the baby to cook as long as she needed to. So instead

I was on strict bed rest for three days, complete with a bedpan and a walker. Nobody saw that part on TV: the show gave us a break and didn't film those last days of my pregnancy. Thanks, Oxygen.

After that, whatever semblance I had of being a mellow mom was gone. I slept cradling Liam's video monitor in my arms. One morning Liam slept until 8:15. I stared at the monitor watching the minutes tick by: 8:16, 8:17. At 8:18 I said to Dean, "This isn't normal. We have to go check on him." Dean said, "He's just tired. He's a baby." I said, "But what if he's dead?" I was sure he was dead. Dean said, "How could he be dead? What would he die from?" I looked at him blankly, then thought about his question. I took a moment to contemplate my answer and was dead serious when I said with utter confidence, "Sometimes people just randomly die."

Yes, random death became my new fear. I'll admit that it wasn't completely rational. But at least worrying that something would happen to one of the children or that something would happen to Dean and as a result my children would live a fatherless life was a little more normal than worrying that the unequal treatment of shampoo bottles in my shower would be the butterfly effect that led to world destruction.

I'd never called Dean, or the boyfriends who preceded him, to say, "Where are you?" or "When are you coming home?" I was never the kind of girlfriend who checked up on her man, and I didn't want or expect to be that kind of wife. But having kids made me become that person for the kids' sake—and my own peace of mind. Just the other day Dean went to drop something off at four p.m. and wasn't home by five. I immediately imagined the worst. Oh my God, his children needed him. Where was he? Was he in a car? Driving? But driving was dangerous. He could die. He was dead. He was dead like a dog on the highway.

I'm the same way about Liam—constantly afraid. I may have been calm about my boyfriends, but with my friends' children I was always the person nobody wanted around, because the second a kid stumbled or scraped himself, I would gasp. You know, that gasp of horror that makes a kid decide he's hurt and scared and should burst into tears right away. Before I had kids I was always apologizing to Jenny or Sara for the gasping.

What's worse, Liam is a speedy little man. He's so fast, I have to be right behind him. When he's running along the sidewalk right in front of our house, I'm trailing after him picturing him tripping and smashing his head on the concrete. When he first learned to trot I was so scared that he was going to fall and crack his head open that I used to put a bike helmet on him. I've worked hard to curtail the use of protective gear. And the gasping, because honestly I'd be gasping twenty-four hours a day and at risk of hyperventilation. When Liam falls, I say, "Yay! Good fall!" Meanwhile my heart is pounding and my blood pressure is off the charts.

As you might imagine, a person who is subject to infinite fears and worries, rational and irrational, doesn't go into child-birth a model of confidence. Actually, I had myself pretty much convinced that this was it. Giving birth to my daughter was how I was going to die. I was destined to end my life like some impoverished wench in a Dickens novel—during childbirth.

Liam was an unplanned cesarean birth, so by the time I went into the operating room, I was exhausted from seventeen hours of labor. There was no time to worry about how surgery would go. There was no choice in the matter. But this time I had months to think about being cut open. I had never researched the procedure the first time. Seriously, people, *they cut your body open.* They cut you open, take your bladder off your uterus, cut your uterus open, and pull out a friggin' baby! Sure, neat trick, but once that stuff is rearranged, how do they know how to put it back? It's not like the game Operation, where there's a loud buzz if you make a mistake. It makes perfect sense that you would die. It makes much more sense than that everything will be fine and you will live out a full, happy life with a beautiful child.

All I kept thinking about was this horror film called *Turistas* with Josh Duhamel where (spoiler alert!) some kids on a bus tour in Brazil get stranded on a remote beach. After they're robbed, they meet a guy who promises to help them, only to find out that their new friends plan to harvest their organs and sell them on the black market. There is a scene where a doctor gives a girl anesthesia, then cuts her open, and while she is still awake, he is taking her organs out and putting them on her stomach. That's what was going to happen to me. So what if my doctor was my friend? Someone was going to push him aside and harvest my organs.

In a way, living with my irrational fears had prepared me for childbirth and motherhood. I was so used to moving forward despite the morbid fantasies that I accepted my fate with resignation—if approaching a cesarean with unmitigated terror can be considered accepting one's fate. This fear of mine wasn't the fault of Mommywood, and it was hard to pin it on my upbringing, though in therapy I tried. It was just who I was and I'd have to protect my kids from the same mind-set as best I could.

My Birthday Girls

The day of my cesarean was upon us. It was June 9, which also happened to be the eleventh birthday of my beloved pug Mimi (you know Mimi!). My daughter and Mimi would have the same birthday. I was (of course) a nervous wreck about the surgery that I was convinced would end my life, but we still had a birthday party for Mimi before we went to the hospital. Isabel, our longtime housekeeper (or dog nanny as she calls herself) made her a cake with eleven candles. Lord knows I love a birthday party, but I can't say I was very gung ho about this one. I was rushing around, trying to pack my bag. Granted, I should have been packed already, but this was number two. I didn't have my act together. We were late to the hospital, and I didn't really want to explain to Dr. J that we were late to surgery because of a dog's birthday party. But she was a very special dog.

I was all worked up about the cesarean, thinking those crazy thoughts I let get the better of me. Outside the operating room, Dr. J tried to reassure me. He said, "You walk to the operating room, get on the table, have an epidural, and half an hour later you'll have your baby girl. It's easy." It sounded simple and civilized, but my heart was pounding so hard that I thought the baby had moved up to my chest and was trying to kick her way out (which, come to think of it, seems as arbitrary and likely as any of the other options). I was weeping. I knew that even if I didn't die, I was never doing this again. It was too horrifying. It wasn't worth it. This was definitely my last child.

It was time. Mehran and my friend Amy, who had come to support me, waited outside the operating room. I bid them farewell, saying, "Good-bye, I love you," as if these were the last words I'd ever exchange with my dearest friends. Dean had to wait outside the door of the operating room while they gave me the epidural. I hadn't expected that; I was counting on Dean's being with me the whole time. But Dr. J held my hands and said, "Just look in my eyes. It's going to be fine." I'm lucky that my doctor happens to be my friend. I'm pretty sure most doctors wouldn't be staring into my eyes and holding my hands. It did cross my mind that locking the surgeon's hands in a death grip wasn't exactly wise. He was going to need those hands to make a precise incision. But I couldn't let go.

The epidural took, Dean came to my side, and then, not much later, I heard my daughter's first cry. It was the best feeling imaginable.

When I was pregnant, Dean and I read through a baby name book with five thousand listings. There wasn't a single name we liked. Naming Liam had been easier than I had expected. When I found out I was having a boy, Dean said, "I've always liked the name Liam," and I said, "I love it." His middle name was Aaron, for my dad. It was that simple. But my whole life I'd wanted to name my baby girl Estella because I loved the book *Great Expectations*. Dean liked the name too. Her middle name would be Doreen for Dean's mother. Estella Doreen McDermott—we thought we were set. We lived with that for a month, but one night I told Dean it didn't sound right. He agreed. Then we thought of Stella. It's Latin for "star," and it was beautiful: Stella Doreen McDermott.

When I heard Stella's little wail, I immediately thought, *I can't wait to get pregnant again!* After all my fear and anguish. That's how it goes: no matter what kind of pain childbirth involves, women are made to forget instantly so that we're willing to keep reproducing.

As with Liam, when Stella cried I felt overwhelming joy. She was there. She was real. I was so excited that I started crying. But then, when they took her over to measure her and do those tests they do, I was struck by a totally new feeling of worry. *Oh my God, when she was inside me I could protect her.* When she was in utero I had control, but now she was out in the world. They had her over there on the scale and I couldn't get to her. I couldn't reach her. I wanted them to give her back to me right away. It struck me that this was what it was going to be like for her whole life. I was going to worry. With Liam I felt pure happiness. Joy, joy, joy. But that underlying fear and worry with Stella hit me heavily. I was going to worry about her more than I worried about Liam.

Was it because she was a girl? Boys could take care of themselves but girls brought a whole new set of worries. I always reflect on that feeling and how my response to the children was different, literally at birth.

When they put Stella in Dean's arms, he started bawling. Dean has always wanted a little girl. He was sobbing uncontrollably. He said, "My daughter. Thank you for giving me my daughter." It made me cry again, and the two of us wept over that precious baby like fools.

When Liam was born, my mother's appearance at the hospital was a huge part of the experience. She and I hadn't spoken since my dad's funeral, and her being there for me was an act of reconciliation. All the same, her presence shifted my focus away from the baby. Was she angry? Was she okay? Was she annoyed that I had too many visitors in the hospital room? What should I talk to her about? This time my mother didn't come, but I felt like my real family was there.

I guess the best way to explain the feeling is this: You know how when you have your closest friends over for dinner, you don't worry about them. If the food's not ready and they're hungry, you know they'll help themselves. But as soon as you go beyond that first circle of friends and entertain people you don't see all the time, it starts to be work. You have to make sure they're comfortable and having a good time. My mother should feel like my real family, closer to me than my circle of friends, but in my case the situation is reversed. My mom is the one I need to make sure is kept comfortable and entertained. But not this time. It was just me, Dean, Mehran, Amy, and by the time the baby was born, Jenny. I didn't feel sad at all. I relaxed and focused on Stella.

We hadn't had time to move into the new house before the baby was born. I was so stressed about it that our amazing friends Scout, Suzanne, Marcel, and James volunteered to oversee the movers and to unpack us while I was in the hospital giving birth to Stella. So we came home to a totally different house with a new family member. It was like Christmas.

When we opened the door of our brand-new suburban dream house and carried four-day-old Stella inside, we were greeted by our cameramen. We were back to work. It may not sound like work, being on a reality show. All you have to do is live your life while other people follow you around with cameras. But it feels like more than that. It means a film crew is in my house and I'm going to be out there for the world to see. With Liam, Dean and I had a nice, long maternity leave to bond with him. Not this time.

The biggest welcome home came from Mimi. She squealed, turned in circles, and waited for me to come over to her bed to introduce Stella. Ever since Liam was first born, Mimi seemed to know that his baby clothes belonged to him. But during my pregnancy as I started to get clothes for Stella, and so many of them were Mimi's signature color—pink—she thought they were for her. When Mimi saw me unwrap a new little pink dress, she sprang to life. She'd run over, excited, as if she assumed I was going to put it on her. The day we came home from the hospital, when we walked through the door, Isabel had dressed Mimi up for our arrival. She was flaunting a beautiful pink cashmere sweater that someone had sent for Stella. I shrugged; eh, we'll wash it. She was so happy. And stylish.

Good Fences Make Good Neighbors

We didn't live in the new house before Stella was born, but we'd already gotten a first taste of the neighborhood. Okay, so I get it that a paparazzi-hounded reality star may not be the "good family neighborhood" dream neighbor. She's probably got too many cars, too much trash, reality show cameramen coming and going at all hours of the night, and a stalker or two on top of it all. Also, she's probably a pretentious snob who doesn't give a crap about her neighbors, leaves shopping bags in her wake, and would be the last person in the world to, say, pick up your newspaper if you were out of town.

From the start, the neighbors were a little skeptical about me and Dean. (I'd be surprised if they were skeptical about Liam.) We did a little work on the house before we moved in—changing the cabinets in the kitchen, putting up wallpaper—

and one neighbor commented to me about the commotion. I was surprised; I think it's pretty common to paint a house before you move in.

But that comment wasn't all. We had considered putting up a small gate in the front of the house. Nothing forbidding—just a low gate to let the paparazzi know exactly where our property line started. Then we decided against it because it was too pricey. Next thing I know, one of my neighbors—let's call him Wally—sent me an email. (I'd given my email to the Fourth of July block party planning committee. Isn't that what good neighbors do?) It was a polite, but forceful email that said something like, "This is a charming, close-knit neighborhood. We understand that you have security issues, but a huge six-foot wall is not only illegal, it will take away from the charm of the neighborhood. And it'd be a shame to put it in because if you do, we're all going to get together with torches and megaphones and baseball bats, march over to your house, and make you take it down." Okay, he may not have mentioned torches. But he did mention a six-foot wall. A six-foot wall? Where did he get that? Welcome to the neighborhood.

I responded with an equally polite email. We actually had decided not to put up a *fence*. And by the way, we were never planning to put up a six-foot anything! Then I added, "Not having a fence puts my safety at risk, but since this is such a tight-knit neighborhood, I just know that when a rabid Donna Martin fan breaks in and you hear my screams, you'll rush to my aid." I fantasized for a minute about sending the email as it was, then deleted the crazed fan part.

The day I got home from the hospital we went back to filming for *Tori & Dean*. The show has a small crew, about five or six people. They show up in a single van. There are no big cameras or extras. It's a pretty small and quiet operation. The crew is always very respectful. When they showed up first thing in the morning, they knocked quietly and asked if the babies were awake. If anyone was still sleeping, they'd hang out on the front lawn until we invited them in. On one of those days Wally stopped our painter and asked if we had a permit to do the show at our house. He said, "It's like they're making a porno." Wally, our personal welcome committee.

When the painter reported this to me, all the air came out of the balloon of my dreams. Dean got really mad. He was pacing around the living room declaring that he wanted to knock on the guy's door and say, "Who do you think you are? I'm moving in with my family. We have a newborn baby. We worked hard to be able to afford to live here. This is the welcome we get?"

I said, "No, you can't! They won't be our friends. They'll hate us. It's my dream!"

Dean was like, "Fuck it, we have friends already."

I said, "We'll kill them with kindness. Once they know us they'll come around." Dean was skeptical, but he didn't do anything. He knew how much it meant to me to fit in.

A week later our neighbors from across the street stopped by to welcome us to the neighborhood. I opened the door to find them standing there with flowers from their garden and home-made brownies. The bad taste of Wally's politely threatening email left my mouth. Neighbors were bringing brownies! I'd only seen such encounters on TV. But I knew what it meant. It meant I really, truly lived in a neighborhood for the first time in my life. Yes, I have to admit I paused for a moment to wonder if they had poisoned the brownies, but that's just me and my irrational fears. It was absolutely no reflection on the perfectly nice, normal people standing at the door waiting to come in. Right. I was a mess. I'd just been nursing Stella. I was in sweats and my hair was a disaster. Stella was wrapped in a blanket. "I'm so sorry the house is such a wreck!" I said as I invited them in. They had a son, Sam, who was close to Liam's age. I hoped that the boys would be friends.

I showed them around the house, which still had stacks of boxes yet to be unpacked and piles of stuff everywhere. They were so pleasant and friendly. I was trying my best to be equally pleasant and friendly. Everyone was doing the right thing, but I could see that they felt weird. I felt weird too. We all felt uncomfortable. It should have been so nice, but something wasn't natural. What was going through their minds? Did they think we were normal or celebrity-warped? Did they wish we hadn't moved in but still dropped by anyway because that's what you do with neighbors? Would they have felt equally uncom-fortable if we were anyone else? Is that just part of meeting the neighbors? Is it always a little awkward? Or was it me: was I the one making it awkward? I'd never done this before. Had

I brought Mommywood to their pleasant neighborhood? Or were they exiling me to Mommywood because that was where we belonged? Everyone moves. Everyone meets neighbors. Most people look for friends—or at least acquaintances—and ways to fit in. But our celebrity brought with it other issues and considerations that had nothing to do with who we were. Was a normal relationship with neighbors possible for us? That whole internal monologue went through my head as I gave them the tour and told them I hoped we'd all get to know one another. Yeah, maybe that's why I didn't come across well. I had a lot going on in my head.

We put the bumpy entry into the neighborhood aside to focus on more important things: decorating. Sure, I wanted the house to be super chic but my big thing was that it had to be cozy and child-friendly. That was the idea, anyway. Then I started designing. I got so excited. It was like Liam's first birthday party all over again. I start off small, but then I get carried away. I couldn't help myself. I had always lived in rentals, so I'd never decorated my own house before. The bed-and-breakfast was my taste, but we worked with a designer who brought us ideas and samples and mostly we said yes or no. This was my first chance to design a house in the style I wanted. As soon as I got going I thought, *Wow, I have great taste!* When I was growing up, wallpaper was unchic. It seemed sort of tacky, like having a furry toilet seat cover. But now I was seeing such amazing new wallpapers. And to me nothing said "This is not a rental" more than wallpaper. I became

wallpaper-obsessed. I would have wallpapered the refrigerator if we hadn't had a budget.

Did I say cozy and child-friendly? Sure, sure, but I'd always dreamed of having a formal living room. It's funny, because when I was growing up we had, like, fifty formal living rooms and they meant nothing to me. But in my adult life I never had a real living room. It was always a living room/family room. Sometimes it was a living room/family room/office. Now we had a separate room that we planned to use as a family room. This was my chance to design the formal living room of my dreams.

I was decorating the house in Hollywood Regency style, a throwback to old Hollywood glamour. I did the living room fireplace in gold and black lacquered wood. There was a velvet tufted couch and an antique Aubusson rug (well, a faux Aubusson). I recovered a set of old leather club chairs—my one concession to the budget. There were light silk drapes with embossed trees. And there was a hint of Asia in the buffet and the prints on the wall. The bar cart was fantastic. It was stocked with etched crystal decanters and highball and shot glasses. Kid-friendly? Not so much.

Okay, so the living room was chock-full of accidents waiting to happen. And, wouldn't you know it, it was Liam's favorite room in the house. All he wanted to do was chase us and be chased around that room. Clearly the first time Liam decided to throw a ball in the house it was going to land smack in the middle of that glassware-filled glass cart. Still, I cherished that space. I pictured myself in a long caftan, with long painted red

nails, reclining on the velvet couch with a tumbler of scotch on the rocks in hand. I loathe scotch, but who cares? I'd twirl it in the glass and just be in heaven.

When the living room was almost complete, I started to panic. Our media room was tiny, and we wanted it to double as a playroom. Maybe we needed the living room to be a place to watch TV. Dean hates TVs. He'd rather not have TVs anywhere, especially in the bedroom or the kitchen. But the house I grew up in had TVs in every room. Dean and I compromised: I agreed not to have a TV in the bathroom, I promised him the TV in the kitchen would be off during family dinners, and I reminded him that he liked the bedroom TV just fine when we were watching porn.

Now it suddenly seemed important that the living room have a TV. A critical anchor for the room. I couldn't help myself. I put a huge TV in, facing the couch. But the truth is that once we settled into the house, we never used the living room TV. Media room TV? Yes. Kitchen TV? Yes. Bedroom TV? Yes. But the living room TV? Never. So in my dream room there's a gigantic TV on the wall as decorative art. It isn't exactly Hollywood Regency. I blew it.

The living room isn't cozy. It isn't family-friendly. We hardly ever use it. But every night before I go to bed I walk past the doorway and stop to look because it's so gorgeous. I turn out the lights, smile, and sigh with self-satisfaction.

At long last it was done. Dean and I, Liam and little Stella were home. And Patsy was back to help care for Stella. For my first postbaby exercise effort I wheeled out the honkin' double baby jogger that was the cornerstone of my suburban fantasy. I strapped on a brand-new pedometer so I could track how far I was running. I found a thermal mug that fit in the jogger's cup holder and filled it with iced coffee. I put on the cutest running outfit I could squeeze my postpartum body into (in case of paparazzi) and put my hair back. I gave both the kids diaper changes, slathered Liam with sunblock and arranged the shade so that Stella wouldn't get a drop of sun. Then I set off on my jog.

A couple of blocks later my legs seemed to stop all by themselves. It dawned on me: *I can't do this!* Another strike against the suburban dream. From now on I would just walk. That would be my exercise. It was better than nothing.

One day, as I was preparing to embark on one of my mega-calorie-burning strolls, our painter came in and said, "That's your neighbor. He just asked me about your wall." I ran to the window to see a man just turning to walk away. So this was Wally—the one-man welcome-to-the-neighborhood committee. He was still asking the painter about the alleged six-foot wall. After I sent him that email saying we weren't building one! He didn't believe me! This guy I had to meet.

Dean and I hurried outside and walked right up to him. Dean said hello and shook his hand. I grabbed him, hugged him, and said, "Oh my God, I'm so excited to finally meet you in person. I'm so glad to be in the neighborhood." The whole time I'd been telling Dean, "We have to kill him with kindness.

I'm telling you. I believe in this." So I hugged Wally, and when I stepped back, I saw his whole facial expression change. The tenseness drained out. It was genius. He was super nice from that moment on. And just like that, hope sprung anew.

I couldn't blame our neighbors for having their doubts about the celebrities next door, but they'd get to know us, we'd get to know them, and soon enough we'd all be playing kickball in the palm-tree-lined streets. Or at least our kids would be while we drank fruity cocktails from a punch bowl. The suburban dream was alive again.

End of an Era

There was an emptiness in our new house. I knew it was coming. I knew it the minute I found out that Stella was going to be born on Mimi's birthday. I knew Mimi was going to die. You know, one life finishes when another one starts, circle of life, all that.

Mimi was a true Hollywood pug. She wore couture clothes, which I kept in a little armoire. She would have it no other way. People chastised me for dressing her, but you have to believe me when I tell you that Mimi felt naked without clothes. When she heard the sound of me opening the armoire, she always came flying, howling with excitement. She loved getting dressed and would push her little front legs through the sleeves. I swear, any doubter who watched me dress Mimi became a believer. Put that pug in a dress and pearls and she was happy.

Mimi starred with me in my series *So NoTORIous* on VH1.

Any time you see a dog in a scripted show, it's a trained dog. Not Mimi. The script would say, "Mimi runs across the room, jumps into Tori's arms, and howls." I'd get nervous. Mimi had many qualities, but obedience wasn't top of the list. Stardom was, however. Mimi hit her mark every time. She was a true performer. As befit a star of her stature, Mimi walked the red carpets (okay, she was carried). The paparazzi would shout, "Over here, Mimi!" and she'd turn, pose, and wait for the flash.

Mimi was a star, but she wasn't immortal. I already knew she was on her way out. She was eleven years old, which is very old for a pug. She was never a very healthy dog. She had problems with her hips, neck, breathing, heart; it's actually amazing how many problems she packed into that little pug body of hers. I always gave her the best medical care I could find—top vets, holistic treatments, acupuncture, water therapy, massage, pain management counseling, and plenty of love. (I'm joking about the pain management counseling. Sort of.)

The morning of Stella and Mimi's birthday (Mimi: eleven, Stella: zero) I'd been a little put out that I had to deal with Mimi's birthday—the cake, putting her in a dress, taking pictures. Seriously, a dog party? On the day I might die in childbirth? But now I thank God I did it. One week later—just three days after we came home from the hospital—I was in pain from my C-section, so though I usually come downstairs with Liam for breakfast, that day I stayed in bed. Patsy brought me Stella whenever she needed to nurse. Around two p.m. I was nestled in bed, and Paola had brought Liam up for a visit.

Liam opened a magazine. There was an ad for our show in it, featuring Mimi. Liam pointed right at her and said, "Mimi! Mimi!" for the first time.

Maybe Liam knew something at that moment that none of the rest of us knew. Soon after that I finally got out of bed to get some lunch. Dean stopped me on the stairs and said, "Mimi died about fifteen minutes ago." I started crying right there on the steps, saying, "No! Mimi was my baby. My life. My everything." It's true, Mimi was raised as a baby, not a dog.

I came downstairs, memories of Mimi flooding my mind. I remembered her sitting in a makeup chair at *So NoTORIous*, eating a bacon and egg breakfast burrito every morning, living the life. I thought about the time Dean and I brought her to a bar and she hung out on a bar stool for hours, just happy to be with me. (She did poop behind the counter. It was a bar. Things happen.) I thought about the time I brought Mimi to the Malibu Country Mart in a bikini. A man saw her and said, "That's disgusting."

I said, "What?"

He said, "You put a dog in a bathing suit. You think she likes that?"

I said, "Of course! She's in Malibu." Mimi absolutely liked to be dressed in a style appropriate to the situation.

Oh, for so long I'd brought Mimi everywhere with me. She was my best companion. I loved her.

All that was true, but I also felt bad about how I'd treated Mimi in her final year, after Liam was born. I know it's normal to pay less attention to a beloved pet when you're pregnant, then taking care of a baby, then doing both at the same time, but I still regret it. I didn't dress her up as frequently. Because of her hips, she could only walk on carpet. When I passed by her little dog bed, she'd whine. I always stopped to pet her, but I wouldn't pick her up and carry her everywhere I went the way I once did. Mimi was by all standards a well-cared-for dog. Our housekeeper Isabel was devoted to her. She walked Mimi and fed her and spent time with her. Still, I wish I'd found a way to give Mimi ten minutes of my complete attention every day. So little time, yet it would have meant so much to her.

Downstairs, on the sofa next to Mimi's still-warm body, I started to melt down. When Nanny died, I wished I'd called her back and seen her more. I told her that in the last phone conversation we had, and she said, "It's okay. Just remember to call your dad. It makes him sad when you don't call." Nanny gave me wisdom that I could use, right then. But when my father died I had the same regret. I hadn't seen him for nine months. I let my discomfort with my mother overshadow all the years I'd had with him, years that meant so much to me. The excuse that I didn't feel welcome only goes so far. I could have barged in and said, "He's my dad. I want to see him. I don't care if I'm not welcome here; I want to see him." I'd been given these two major opportunities to learn from my mistakes, but I'd gone ahead and repeated this mistake for a third time. Not holding Mimi for ten minutes a day was equivalent—on a dog level—to not calling Nanny or my father. I felt extreme guilt. I don't stay in touch with the people (and in this case, dog) I love most in the world, and then they die. I could have done more, I should have done more, and now it was too late.

Mimi was a Hollywood star, and she deserved a Hollywood funeral. I know what you're thinking: a memorial for a dog?—must be just another excuse for Tori to host a theme party. But the truth is that I was dreading the memorial. I don't love dealing with feelings; part of me just wanted to move on. Mimi was gone. It was time to let go. Then I thought about how much Mimi loved attention, parties, and publicity. She was such a grand dame. I knew she would have wanted a big party with crowds of people paying their respects. And I knew there were many people who needed a place and a community of fellow mourners to grieve their loss. If my dog Ferris passed away, I wouldn't think of throwing a memorial party. That's not his style. Ferris would be embarrassed at all the fuss. But Mimi—Mimi had to go out in style.

Okay, I'll admit it: once I was committed to hosting such an event, my party-planning passion kicked in. Mimi's memorial took place at a Zen tea garden in West Hollywood called Dr. Tea's. It was the same spot (though the name had changed) where we had had Liam's baby shower. And, yes, there was a theme. So sue me. Mimi's signature color was pink, so everybody came to the memorial dressed in pink. There were passed hors d'oeuvres—deviled eggs because they were her favorite—as well as pink cocktails and pink flowers on the tables. For all my reservations about the memorial service, once I was there, it was so beautiful and I felt so happy and was a little bit teary with the knowledge that Mimi was smiling down on it, loving her last moment in the spotlight.

After half an hour of cocktails, everyone gathered to watch a video tribute on a big screen. There was footage from her appearances on our show and still shots—Mimi on the lawn of our bed-and-breakfast; Mimi in my lap; Mimi lying on my pregnant belly; Mimi in a dress with boots—all set to music. Oh Liam and Stella, just you wait. There is nothing I love more than a video montage.

Every celebrity with a heart should commit to a charity she believes in. Mimi was an unofficial mascot of Much Love Animal Rescue, an animal shelter I work with all the time. Mimi regularly attended Much Love events. Her openness about her roots as a pet store puppy and about the health issues she had faced her whole life brought awareness to the problems of dogs who are inbred and poorly treated in puppy mills and pet stores everywhere. Dean came forward to read a letter from the head of Much Love. Then he announced that we were establishing the Mimi La Rue Fund for sick and injured animals in conjunction with Much Love. There were "puggybanks" on all the tables where people could make donations.

Jenny's husband, Norm, had sent us a poem called "Rainbow Bridge" about the doggy afterlife, which Dean read. Then Mehran came forward and asked everyone to lift a glass of pink champagne. Mehran used to housesit for us sometimes. He always says, "Even when I came home late, disheveled and reeking of a bar, Mimi would still cuddle. Oh, the things that Mimi saw—and she still loved me." But at that moment, when Mehran got up to make his toast, he was so nervous that he started by saying, "Mimi was a person who was a friend of mine." Person? Jenny and I were in the front row and chuckled. It lightened a sad moment.

Everyone was handed a little pink box. A speaker from Agape—a trans-denominational spiritual center—read a prayer, and after the prayer she asked everyone to open their boxes. Inside each box was a monarch butterfly. We released them and they all flew out into the sky.

The famous pet psychic Sonya Fitzpatrick had done a reading with Mimi once for *Entertainment Tonight*. I thought maybe she could come to the service, but she wasn't available. Someone recommended another psychic, who specialized in connecting with loved ones who'd crossed over. She could work with people or animals, and she agreed to come.

After the service I spoke privately with the pet psychic. I told her about my guilt. I thought now that there were two babies in the house, Mimi felt unwanted and gave up on life. I wanted to know if Mimi had died of heartbreak. The psychic saw it differently (go figure). She said, "No, Mimi was waiting for the right moment to go. It was meant to be. Mimi and Stella had an agreement before Stella was born. A bond. This was Mimi's time. She left this world knowing that Stella would be there for you. You'll see, when Stella can speak, you'll see that she knows who Mimi is."

Mimi was so tired in the end. She had trouble walking. She had no zest for life. She was just lying there. After talking to the psychic, I felt that Mimi had been hanging on just long enough to see me through Stella's birth. Mimi thought she was my protector. She knew I'd have a girl. She was willing to let the girl take her place. She waited for Stella to come. Once I had my little girl, I was happy and she could pass knowing things were going to be okay.

In a back room, just for the family, Mimi was resting in an open casket, pink of course. She was laid out in her favorite pink dress and pearls, surrounded by flowers. We brought Ferris in to say good-bye. I took some time alone with her.

Mimi was my first baby, and even though I got most of my opinions about parenting (positive and negative) from Nanny and my parents, it was with Mimi that I got some real, hands-on practice. I remember one Halloween I brought Mimi to the set of *90210* (Mimi always went to the set with me). I started to dress her in her Halloween costume. She was going as a prima ballerina. But Mimi, who usually loved nothing more than a fancy new outfit, especially a pink one, was not having any of it that morning. As I tried to slip her tiny paws through the petite sleeves, she was struggling and crying and making it harder on both of us. I didn't want to force her to get dressed. She usually got so excited about it. But here it was, Halloween, the one day of the year when dressing up was really important (to me, anyway), and she picked this of all days to decide to be an ordinary, clothes-resistant dog? Time was ticking. I was late to work, and I hated to be late. I had a meltdown. I shouted, "Mimi, be still! You're being a bad girl!"

Mimi instantly cowered and went submissive. I got her outfit on, but now I was the one who was crying. I drove to work with tears running down my face. At work I sat in the makeup chair tormented by what I'd done. She was a dog. I had no business forcing her to wear clothes, and I had yelled at her! I never yelled at Mimi (which may explain why she was never exactly housebroken). As they attempted to fix my mascara, I wailed, "I'm a bad mom! I'm a bad mom!" I was devastated. Being a mom one day was so important to me, and I knew Mimi was my practice child. I could just see myself trying to dress my own baby, having a mental breakdown, and screaming at him. A person like me couldn't have children. I'd scar them for life. I was literally in hysterics. The makeup people finally gave up and sent me to get my hair done. They'd try again later.

I've never forgotten that episode. When Liam twists and writhes, not wanting his diaper changed, I have all the patience in the world. When he throws his spoon to the floor time after time, I calmly pick it up and ask if he's done eating. When he isn't ready to get out of the pool, I remind him of all the fun things we have to do at home. I still have to work at it sometimes, but Mimi taught me patience.

Mimi saw me through a complete chapter of my life. She was there for me in my twenties. I think of those years as the time when I was really growing up and becoming an adult, and Mimi went through everything with me. Bad boyfriends, breakups, friends, my party days. We'd all come home drunk and curl up with Mimi on the couch. Mimi saw it all. Mimi was there through my first marriage, my divorce, my second marriage, my first pregnancy, Liam's birth, my second pregnancy. It was as if she recognized that I was completely formed, married and settled. There were no more major ups and downs to come. Her work here was done. The Mimi years were the years that made me the woman I am today.

I said my last good-byes and kissed her. I closed the casket and they took her away to cremate her.

People magazine posted news of Mimi's death in their obituary section. Not long after Mimi died, Dean and I were in a restaurant and the waiter said, "I'm sorry to bring it up, but my friends and I are huge fans of Mimi La Rue and we were really sad to hear about your loss." Mimi was a true star, a paparazzi sweetheart. I know she is missed.

At her memorial, the pet psychic said that Mimi will come back in some form to let me know things are okay. Ten minutes after all the butterflies that we released flew out of the tea garden, I saw one last butterfly fluttering around near Stella and said, "Look! It's Mimi." Maybe it was Mimi, who can say?

Isabel, who loved Mimi so much, has transferred her devotion to Stella. She truly believes there's a connection. She'll say, "Look how good she looks in pink. Like Mimi!" and, "Oh, Stella wears little dresses. Like Mimi!" Isabel is so sweet that I never have the heart to say what I'm thinking in my head, *Yeah, um, lots of baby girls look cute in pink and wear little dresses.* But every so often I see a monarch butterfly in our backyard. That seems unusual to me: I haven't seen a ton of monarch butterflies in my daily life, and I'd never seen one in the backyard of any house I lived in (and a couple of those backyards were big enough to qualify as nature preserves). I look at the butterfly, watching it flit here and there in its peaceful journey, and I can't help wondering if that's Mimi, telling me it's all going to be all right.

When's the Baby Due?

A week after Mimi's memorial, when Stella was two weeks old, Dean and I went out for our first lunch since her birth. I was still healing from the cesarean section and hadn't begun to think about the baby weight and how and when I was going to get rid of it. I didn't have unrealistic expectations for how I should look two weeks after giving birth, but I knew other people did. When I say other people I mean the media. It was a given that how much weight I'd gained and lost and how quickly it came and went (or didn't go) was going to be public fodder. People on the street would check me out, maybe whisper to one another. The paparazzi would swarm to get the least flattering shots. They would sell the photos to magazines, that would then present my postbaby body for everyone else's judgment. It feels a lot like construction workers staring at my tits, but more intense. As if every thought that a construction worker had was posted on a giant billboard for the world to see. For some reason people think it's acceptable to judge women's bodies as if they're show ponies. And I guess by posing on red carpets I've made myself fair game for the less flattering versions of that spectacle. I've signed on to that lifestyle.

I flashed back to a day when Liam was three months old. Most people who knew that I'd been pregnant now knew that Liam had been born. I was in the market, and a woman said, "I recognize you. When's the baby due?" Before I could answer, she grabbed my belly. My three months postpartum jelly belly. I wasn't ready to look at it in the mirror, much less offer it up for stranger grabbing. The perpetrator (okay, maybe she was the victim) released her grasp, realizing instantly that the baby had moved out; I started my diet that night.

Now, getting ready for lunch at La Scala, I took at least an hour to get dressed. I tried on dress after dress looking for the one that would hide everything and offer me the best protection possible from belly grabbers and judging cameras. Maybe I should have been looking in the "tent" drawer. If I had had a "tent" drawer. I don't think Fred Segal has a tent division.

Indeed, I was right to be worried. This time there was no belly-grabbing incident, but Dean and I had barely touched our appetizers before the paparazzi found us. I could just see the headlines. Would it be "Tori Spelling Pregnant Again?—Or Just Fat?" Or would they compare me to other celebrities who had recently given birth: "Mirror, Mirror on the Wall, Who Gained the Most Baby Weight of All?"

As we left La Scala to walk to our car, I tried to suck in my belly, but I couldn't really do it. I'd had a C-section. My brain was like, *Stomach muscles? What stomach muscles?* So instead I held my breath, stuck my butt out, and leaned back, contorting my body into a silhouette I imagined would downplay the pooch. When we got to the car, I turned to Dean and said, "I'm about to pass out. I've been holding my breath for two minutes straight."

Postbaby bodies are what they are. The newborn is the priority, and it's all we moms can do to try to get enough sleep. It's natural to want your former body back, but whether or how soon you can do anything about it is different for everyone. In the world of news magazines, however, Hollywood is supposedly full of celebrities who are back in tip-top shape minutes after the baby lets out its first cry.

It just can't be true—there must be corsets and bulge-hiding designer clothes involved—but it's hard for me not to feel competitive with the other celebrities who had babies in the same time frame as I did. Jessica Alba's baby was born at Cedars—the same hospital where Stella was born—two days before I gave birth. I was still recovering from my cesarean, and the idea of doing a sit-up was absolutely terrifying, when photos of Jessica Alba in a bikini appeared in magazines. The article said she was working out six days per week, and I have to say she looked fantastic. But Oh. My. God. The pressure was on. Brooke Burke was three months before me. Nicole Kidman was one month after. They all seemed to immediately revert to their former fabulous bodies. I was relieved and glad to see pictures of Gwen Stefani wearing baggy clothes. Of course she should be wearing baggy clothes, her baby was only one month old! These people are in the same business as I am and we're having babies at the same time. But why exactly do I feel like we have to reattain our prebaby bodies on the same schedule? Because the weeklies tell me I should!

Ah, Mommywood, and the race to lose the baby weight. Two months after Stella was born, Dean and I were having a late afternoon cocktail (yes, I pumped and dumped) on the patio at the Four Seasons. It was so decadent. Like the good old days. A woman and her husband walked up and were about to sit down near us when I saw her gesture toward me. She said to her husband, "We can't sit here. I want to have a cigarette, and she's pregnant." I was sitting in a booth wearing a baggy dress (from the theoretical "tent" drawer). She had no idea who I was, but she could still see that belly of mine and had no doubt that I was expecting. It was time to get to work.

I was never a scale girl, but when I finally started trying to lose weight, I got scale-obsessed. Soon after the Four Seasons trauma, Liam and I were in the bathroom—I'd just finished brushing his teeth—when I stepped on the scale. I'd been eating well for a week and hadn't gotten on the scale for a few days, so I was expecting to see a loss. No such luck. Instead, when I saw the number I said, "Ugh. I'm a beast!" This was just when Liam was starting to pick up phrases, and sure enough, seconds later I heard, "A beast!" I turned around and Liam was saying it and pointing at me.

The next day we were having a big brunch at Barney Green-grass in Beverly Hills with friends and friends of friends. Liam was in a high chair at the table. There was a lull in the conversation when Liam piped up. He said, "A beast!" and he laughed and pointed at me. I was embarrassed in front of the people I didn't know very well and went completely overboard explaining why my son was calling me names. On the other hand, my child was picking up new words. Genius! Let's hope that's the only time I feel proud of being called a beast.

It was just plain hard to relax and take my time losing the weight when nobody else seemed to think that approach was okay. All the attention to the baby weight was getting to me. It actually affected how I saw my own body and what I expected of myself. I'm so conditioned to think I have to look a certain way. Recently a woman came up to me and complimented me on how I looked. She said, "How did you lose all your baby weight?" I said, "No, look, I still have a belly. And Stella is four months old." She said, "Are you kidding? It's been seven years and I'm still trying to lose my baby weight. You look great!" It had been seven years for her, and here I was apologetic about my belly, like it was a public offense. How insane is that? I wanted to say I was sorry for apologizing, but that's a loop I always try to avoid.

The self-consciousness may seem funny considering that on my TV show I let the crew film me in various states of makeup-free reality. I was even okay being filmed four days after Stella was born. I knew going into that taping that it was the worst

I'd ever look. I figured, that's life, and the people who were watching the show knew it. When I watch reality shows, I'm not looking at women's weight.

But magazines are different. Both reality shows and magazines are supposed to capture reality. But judging is part of what magazine readers do. If I see a reality show star in a magazine compared to someone else wearing the exact same dress, I would definitely judge who wore it better. If I'm wearing a dress and I'm standing next to Paris Hilton, in the same dress, who do you think wins? I weigh thirty pounds more than she does. Of course she wears it better! In the magazines I feel scrutinized. I have to have the right outfit. I have to be standing in the right posture. My body has to look perfect. My hair has to be done. I care what they write about me. Maybe I shouldn't, but I do. And caring about it means I try to control it. Oh, if only moms were judging. Then I might have a fighting chance. Or at least a good seven years to lose the baby weight.

My First and Last Block Party

Back home, in our neighborhood, I hoped to leave the celebrity spotlight and all my self-consciousness behind. When we bought our suburban fantasy house, one of the selling points was the Fourth of July block party. What could better represent the normal, all-American childhood I was so determined to give my kids than an old-style July Fourth block party? When I'd gotten a flyer in the mailbox about the block party—before we even moved in—I'd immediately filled out the attached form (so official!) to sign up for the planning committee.

We were new to the neighborhood. I wanted to make a good impression. The block party was my chance to show my neighbors that we were normal, that we and our children fit in here. I wanted to do everything perfectly, to the letter. I was convinced that any mistake I made would be blamed on who I was. I had no idea what preconceptions my neighbors had, but chances were that the first association they had with the name "Tori Spelling" wasn't "down-to-earth mom." Being a happy, enthusiastic participant in the big event was my best chance at showing them who I was.

The planning committee sign-up form should have clued me in. It was a highly organized event. I've been to weddings that were less organized than the Beaver Avenue Block Party. Heck, I may have even had one myself. The emails started coming at least three months in advance of the day. There were July 4, 2008, Beaver Avenue Block Party T-shirts to be designed, ordered, and handed out before the big day. There were activities to be planned, food to be organized, rentals to be arranged.

As soon as we agreed that one of the activities could happen in front of our house, we got our assignment: we were to host the egg toss. Then the Official Beaver Block Party Schedule came. It said that Dean McDermott would host the Beaver Block Party Triennial Egg Toss at 2:15 p.m. I was worried about organizing the egg toss, but then I realized, here's everything you need in order to host an egg toss: eggs. But I was so concerned about getting it right that I still found a way to get all up in my head about it. How many eggs should I buy? What kind of eggs? Did they have to be organic? Cage-free? With omega-3s added? The Organizing Committee's email response calmly told me not to worry about the eggs. They would supply the eggs. When I asked if I should get prizes they said, "Oh no, we have prizes." Apparently hosting the Beaver Block Party Triennial Egg Toss simply meant allowing it to take place in front of our house. Not on our front lawn, but on the street in front of our front lawn. Our job was to be there to witness it. Still, I lost some sleep over the egg toss. Why was there nothing to do? Was the egg toss for newbies? Was that why it had been assigned to us? Did we look too lame to handle the moon bounce? I came from a family that had Christmas snow in Los Angeles. I could handle a moon bounce rental! I guess that's what happens when you invite a natural-born party planner to a highly organized event and then tell her she doesn't have to do anything. It's like bringing a diabetic to an ice cream shop. It's just plain cruel.

As the day approached, the preparations escalated. A week before the event the Distribution Committee distributed decorations for each house and supplemental decorations for the wagons the children would ride in the block-long parade. Every house was supposed to bring one dessert for the potluck table; I planned to make my famous red velvet cake. The night of July 3 all the necessary egg toss supplies were deposited on our doorstep. No surprises. Just eggs.

The morning of July Fourth—the big day!—I sprang out of bed, ready to embrace our retro-cool summer festivities. I dressed the kids in red, white, and blue outfits. We decorated Liam's wagon with the regulation streamers we'd been given. I tried to wrap the trees outside the house with the regulation crepe paper, but the Scotch tape I used to hold it in place failed miserably.

My red velvet cake was ready on the counter, and I set about decorating it with white frosting, blueberries, and strawberries to make an American flag on top. I knew it would be a perfect combination of patriotic and delicious. I had just put the finishing touches on the flag when I reread the Block Party Potluck Table Instructional Email. It explicitly said that all desserts must be cut up into serving-sized pieces. I panicked. I had to cut up my beautiful cake! Pretty as it was, I knew people were looking for us to do things wrong. I had to follow the instructions perfectly or I'd never be accepted.

I grabbed a knife, held my breath, and cut the cake. The second I touched the knife to it, the whole thing collapsed. It was a mess. I was in tears. How could I give my kids a quintessential American childhood if I couldn't even deliver a homemade cake to a neighborhood potluck? Dean walked into the kitchen and was shocked. "Why did you cut it? It looked so beautiful!"

I pointed to my computer. "I just followed the instructions. The Block Party Potluck Table Instructional Email. It said you had to cut it." I returned to the collapsed cake, salvaged what I could, and arranged it into little squares. I flattened the frosting and rearranged the berries. It looked . . . okay. Unlike in the National Anthem, our flag was *not* still there. But the patriotic colors were. Except where the red bled into the white and was kind of pink. Sigh. It wasn't special, but I might not be forever ashamed to show my face on the block.

Our neighbors started setting up for the parade. It was straight out of the fifties. Dogs frolicked on the bright green squares of lawn in front of each house. Dads and kids were working together to hang American flags. Somebody had a megaphone. People started putting out plastic woven lawn chairs so they could sit and watch the parade go by. Uh-oh. I stopped short. I'd invited a bunch of friends to the block party, but I didn't know about the lawn chairs! There was no Block Party Lawn Chair Instructional Email! By chance I had two folding beach chairs with drink holders and everything. I had owned them even before I moved to Beaver Avenue. I was very proud of that. But what about my friends? If we wanted to fit in with the crowd, they definitely needed lawn chairs! I sent out a frantic email to my friends: "Make sure you bring sun hats, lotion, and *lawn chairs.*" Jenny wrote back right away. "I'm sorry, who are you? Did you just ask me to bring a lawn chair to your house? Because (a) I don't own one, and (b) I'm pretty sure you don't have one, and (c) I'm not even sure you know what a lawn chair is. Is this the new suburban you?" Clearly I was in a bad way, because all I could think when I read that was, *In the time it took her to write that snarky email she could have gone to Target and bought some lawn chairs!*

An hour later, Jenny, Mehran, Sara, Amy, Bill and Scout, Suzanne, and Gueran were all at our house, ready for the big party. I showed off my lawn chairs to Jenny.

At ten in the morning the parade began. All the kids and dogs were dressed in matching red, white, and blue Beaver Avenue Fourth of July T-shirts. "Born on the Fourth of July" blared on a staticky sound system. Waving flags, kids pulling wagons with their younger siblings in them, the group started at one end of Beaver and marched to the other end. Hello, Mayberry. My stepson, Jack, pulled Liam in his festooned wagon. Liam waved the whole time. He loved it. Ten minutes later they reached the other end of Beaver. Parade over, on to the next activity.

There were other activities—square dancing, tug-of-war, face painting. One house had an exhibit showing photos of Beaver Avenue and its houses in the seventies. That's when I realized that they've been doing these same block parties since the seventies. When I looked closely at the photos, I saw that it was the same street, lined with the same trees, the same houses . . . and the same people. I actually recognized my neighbors— some as children, some as adults—in the photos. It was incredibly sweet, even if it reminded me a little of that creepy photo at the end of *The Shining*. Still, it made me realize they'd all lived on the same block for a very long time. No wonder they were so worried that we might put up a wall. No wonder they were put off by our camera crew of four. They had to protect the Beaver Avenue Twilight Zone where nothing and nobody ever changes.

Unfortunately, my block party performance anxiety had just begun. Dean suddenly developed a horrible migraine—must have been the incredibly exhausting parade walk—and went back inside to lie down. But, but . . . it said on the email that he was the official egg toss host! It said so on the flyers! (We ourselves had never specified Dean as the family representative, but I guess the husbands were the designated hosts.) As 2:15 approached I went into full panic mode. Dean was still upstairs. What if we were the only house that was late to begin our activity? Tori Spelling—Block Party failure! I was doomed. Thinking fast, I herded all our friends into the front yard. I had to drag Mehran away from the *Vogue* magazine he was reading comfortably in our den. If we didn't have Dean to lead the show, we'd at least compensate with a large, enthusiastic crowd of egg toss supporters. I lined my friends up and prodded them until they had sufficiently welcoming smiles.

At 2:10—with just minutes to spare—Dean showed signs of life. I heard him grumble and ran upstairs. "Dean! It's time for the egg toss, come on!" He stumbled to the bathroom. Would he make it downstairs in time? At 2:13 he came downstairs, fastening his belt on the way. I pushed him out the front door. Okay! We were psyched and ready. The crowd, moving as one well-organized mass, was approaching. Tick, tick, tick. It was 2:15 on the dot. All systems were go. We made it! I breathed a sigh of relief.

Just as the egg toss contestants arrived, an announcement came through the megaphone. The keeper of the megaphone was Wally, the fence-monitoring neighbor who had turned nice when I hugged him. Suddenly, our now-nice neighbor announced, "The fire department!" We all looked up the block. Indeed, two big red fire trucks were at that moment rounding the corner. Like soldiers, the crowd turned away from our house as one unit and ran toward the gleaming fire engines. (They stopped looking like soldiers as soon as they started climbing all over the fire engines.) I was like, "Come on, guys, have you never seen a fire truck before?" But they were gone. All that was left in our yard was us, our friends, and twenty-four eggs. The egg toss was officially postponed.

Per the Block Party Potluck Table Instructional Email, the deadline for delivery of all desserts, precut, was 6:00 p.m., Pacific time. Mehran went with me for the presentation of the cake. We walked to the table—a card table in the middle of the street (provided, presumably, by someone who had been assigned "Beaver Avenue July Fourth Potluck Table" much as we were assigned "Beaver Avenue July Fourth Egg Toss").

On the table were four other desserts. They were store-bought. And they were sitting there in pristine condition. Not one of them had been savagely cut into unattractive, portion-sized pieces. I was aghast. My cake . . . I'd even bought a plastic silver tray for it. It would have been a shining star.

I had no choice but to submit my cake as it was. I looked around, but there was nobody to whom I could present it. No reception committee to whom I could at least explain how hard I'd tried. Even worse—as I looked around I realized that there was nobody on the entire street. All day long people had been bustling around, hanging decorations, chatting across yards, coming in and out of their houses. But right now, at the moment of judgment, the streets were empty. You know how when you're in a café and you put money in the tip jar, you kind of want someone to see you do it? This was like that, but on a much bigger scale. I needed these people to know how much I'd tried, how much I'd worked on this cake and fretted over the rules, how much I'd done everything I possibly could to fit in, to participate, to be a good neighbor. But no one was around. Nobody cared. "Come on," said Mehran, "put it down." But I couldn't.

"We have to wait," I hissed. "Somebody has to see that I participated." After five minutes Mehran was like, "Let's go."

"But they won't know I brought cake."

"You'll know," said Mehran. I think we both knew that wasn't the point.

A couple of hours later, when it was all over, and all the friends left, and the cleanup committee was efficiently clearing the block of any sign of the festivities, I took stock of the day. Cut or uncut, my cake had been eaten. Fire department notwithstanding, the delayed egg toss had been a success. Were my expectations too high? Had I wanted something from the block party that it couldn't possibly give me? If trying hard and following all the rules didn't make me fit in, what would? Was I trying *too* hard? Or did I have to have grown up on this block to feel comfortable here? I looked down at my Beaver Avenue Block Party beer cozy and sighed. So this was neighborhood life. It was very stressful.

Hollywood Halloweens

July Fourth was a bust, but there was still hope. Hallow-een was just around the bend. Halloween was always my favorite holiday—as soon as I was allowed to choose my own costume. That is, when I was an adult. When I was a kid, as with my birthday parties and pretty much everything else, my mother's preferences dominated. And my mother's prefer-ences were always over-the-top. My brother and I wore Hal-loween costumes that were custom-made by Nolan Miller, the costume designer for *Dynasty* and most of my dad's other glamorous shows. They were beautiful costumes, but I can still feel the weight of my Marie Antoinette wig every time I get a headache.

In all my childhood we never had a trick-or-treater come to our house. I longed to see the kids in costumes, to hold out a bowl of candy, but no child in his right mind would have come up such a long driveway. And that was the house we lived in *before* my parents moved to the Manor. Now, for the first time in my life, I lived in a real Halloween neighborhood. My family would have the costumes I dreamed of. We'd have a Halloween party. We'd share a classic Halloween.

A week or so before Halloween we saw Sam, the five-year-old boy who lives across the street, in his front yard with his grandmother. Sam was dressed in a superhero costume. He was very proud of it and was flying all around the yard to show off, with Liam chasing excitedly behind. The superhero's grandmother confessed that she'd made his costume and he wouldn't take it off. The costume was a pair of long johns with purple underwear—the purple version of tighty whities—pulled over it. She'd sewn a superhero-type letter on his shirt and attached a cape. He was wearing a mask she'd cut out of double-layered felt. It was charmingly handmade-looking.

I loved that the grandmother made the costume, in part because the idea of my mother sitting down at a sewing machine to make something for Liam was amusingly absurd. But I also thought about how inexpensive store-bought costumes are these days, and how those long johns alone probably cost her just as much as a store-bought costume. Clearly, that wasn't the point. I'm sure she wanted to take the time to make the costume herself because to her, a homemade costume— that was love. For my mother, maybe those elaborate custom costumes were love (and if love is measured by the height of the wig, she loved me a *lot*). And now, for me, being able to say,

"Look Liam, your store-bought bee suit is right here, inside its plastic shrink-wrap"—that was love. You see, all I ever wanted growing up was store-bought simplicity. And so buying Liam a normal costume from Pottery Barn, a costume like any other kid might wear, a costume that wasn't made by a famous costume designer—there's nothing better to me. And that's part of why I bought myself the adult version of Liam's jenky polyester bee suit. We were going to be matching store-bought bees together. Now *that* was love.

That was the plan for Stella too. I wanted her to be a ladybug, since we call her "Ladybug" or "Buggy," but when I tried to put her in the little red spotted bunting costume I bought for her, she rejected it. She wasn't going for the leg restriction of the bunting bag. Stella's a kicker.

I had learned my lesson about forcing Halloween costumes—first from my mother, who simply never asked what we wanted, and later from Mimi, when I lost my temper trying to force her into her ballerina outfit. The day before Halloween found me running around trying to find Stella a costume that she'd tolerate. I found two different ladybug costumes at two different stores, but both were too big on Stella, so that night I got to work. I attached the wings from one costume and the tutu from another to a red onesie. And when I say *attached,* I mean that I *sewed* the costume together. That's right. I, Tori Spelling, both bought *and* home-made my daughter's first Halloween costume. And if that isn't true proof of some big Halloween love, I don't know what is.

Once the onesie body and the soft little headband with antennae were ready, all I needed were some black tights to complete the costume. The next morning—Halloween—I ran out to get them. Black tights. How hard could that be? Doesn't every infant need black tights at some point? When the costume stores didn't have them, I went—well, I went to the only place that sprang to mind: Kitson Kids on Robertson in Beverly Hills, trendy boutique to the stars.

Kitson Kids sells baby Uggs. They have mini True Religion jeans. They have Little Marc Jacobs dresses, and crib shoes designed to look like leopard satin high heels. Basically, if you want your kid to look like he or she belongs on the fashionable sidewalks of Beverly Hills, Kitson Kids is the place for you. They showed me the pink faux leopard fur coat. The crystal-encrusted pink Uggs. The hair accessories—every hand-crafted baby barrette known to man for the two hairs on Stella's head. The Splendid leggings (but none in black!) for forty-eight dollars. You know, all the celebrity baby staples. Aren't black tights a celebrity baby staple? Apparently not.

I finally found the tights at a shoe store, assembled the costume, and I have to say the result was damn cute. Stella even tolerated her headband. That's my girl—born knowing that the outfit is nothing without the accessories.

In the afternoon, Liam's best friend, Ollie, had a Halloween party. Dean and I brought Liam, Stella, and Jack, who went as a gothic vampire. Dean was dressed as a gladiator/Hercules-type person, and I, of course, was a bee. When Ollie's dad opened the door, he oohed over the kids appropriately. Then he looked at me and Dean and said, "Wow. Kudos. You get an A plus." I smiled: our efforts had paid off! You see, I wasn't just dressed in my store-bought bee costume. I had yellow and gold shimmer eyeshadow. I had black and gold false eyelashes on. My fingernails were painted black. I was wearing a bright yellow wig with black bangs. (I know, quite the find. It went perfectly with my bee costume.) We had good costumes. Cool. I beamed with pride.

That feeling lasted about two minutes. As soon as we stepped into the party, I realized that we weren't the parents wearing the best costumes. We were the *only* parents wearing costumes. No wonder we got an A plus. No one else completed the assignment. My pride immediately turned to indignation. Couldn't they stick something on? A witch's hat? Cat ears? Why didn't they dress up? It was just sad. How about a little effort, people?

As the party went on, my disappointment in the other parents gradually turned into mild self-consciousness, then full-fledged embarrassment. As I had for Stella, I had combined two costumes to achieve my perfect bee outfit. One was an oversized, foamy bee suit with black tights, a headband, and wings. (That was the costume that matched Liam's.) Then I had the stripper version of a bee. That's right. Some costume designer came to work one day and had the brilliant idea of making a stripper bee. It's a completely ridiculous concept. (Stripper nurse, okay. Stripper bee? It's a tough scenario to imagine.) Anyway, the stripper bee was a tight, low-cut costume with a short black tutu. I wore the stripper bee body over a black turtleneck and opaque black leggings, which toned it down from slutty to cute. I wore the wings from the big foamy bee suit. But that wasn't all. In addition to the false eyelashes, the black fingernails, and the wig in bee palette, I also had black and yellow legwarmers and—I was so proud of having found them—black and yellow striped heels. I was carrying a fuzzy purse that said "Honeypot." I wasn't just the girl with the witch's hat. I'd clearly invested a lot of time and thought in my costume. It was starting to feel like a little much.

Then a few moms asked, "When did you have your daughter?" and I started worrying that in addition to being overdone, the costume was also too tight. I thought I had covered my bases by putting the turtleneck and leggings underneath the stripper bee. Had that not done the job? Did I look like a whore? Were these moms judging me? Whenever I feel judged, I feel like there's an extra layer of judgment. I'm not just some wacky mom in a stripper bee costume. That's who I want to be. Instead, I'm *Tori Spelling* in a stripper bee costume. I'm cocktail party joke material. Now I felt like a jackass (a bee-ass? a jack-bee?) and wanted to leave.

Meanwhile, Liam's costume wasn't playing exactly as I had planned either. Stella was fine. She looked adorable, and let's just say she wasn't the only ladybug in attendance. But Liam—well, the little boys at this particular Halloween party were all in much more studly outfits. One boy was David Beckham. He had fake tattoos, hip soccer shorts, and a shirt that said, "I love Victoria." Our host, Ollie, was a golfer. Ollie had on a bow tie, argyle socks, a hat, and sported a mini golf bag. Then there was Liam. My little Pottery Barn bee in a big, fuzzy costume (at least I found him black and yellow Nikes, which gave him a modicum of studliness). Liam was only one and a half. Did he really have to start dressing like a boy? Couldn't I hold on to the animal costumes for a little while longer? Apparently not. As if picking up on the testosterone-fueled disapproval of his peers, Liam started to hate his stuffy little costume, and given my Marie Antoinette history, I wasn't about to force him to wear it. My Halloween fantasy wasn't off to a good start, but I still had hope.

After the Halloween party we came home, where we were going to have a little party with friends before trick-or-treating up and down the block. The dining room was decorated with all sorts of spooky paraphernalia. I made a pumpkin full of chili, and evil eggs. (Get it? Instead of deviled eggs?) There were ghost cupcakes. I had gone to the farmers' market to find the same caramel apples with candy corn and gumdrop faces that my mom used to get for me. And as a finishing touch I used a huge plastic cauldron as a drink bucket, ready with chilled Diet Coke, Sprite, Sunkist, Veuve Clicquot, and Mott's for Tots juice boxes. It was a well-stocked cauldron.

We were ready. Would my friends at least show up in costume? Or would I have to accept that I was an overdone bee slut and let it rain on my Halloween parade? Sara and her daughter, Emma, showed up first. Sara was all in black. No costume. But I could have predicted that Sara wouldn't dress up. She was pregnant, and I knew she was the type to think it was silly anyway. Then Jenny and her family walked in. Jenny, who is also the type you'd think wouldn't be dressed up, was in a full-on Cinderella costume. Oh my God. She was perfect. The headband, the long dress. Her own beautiful blonde hair. As she stood at the door, I could see a couple of little girls out on the street staring at her with open mouths. They were in love. I said, "You could work at Disneyland!" Dean said, "You look hot!" Jenny said, "Target, five dollars." I said, "Settle down, Dean."

Jenny's husband, Norm, was dressed as a surgeon. They have three kids and they still got it together enough to dress up. Thank God for Jenny and Norm. My faith in humanity was restored.

The rest of the party was my gays: Mehran, Gueran, Bill and Scout. I've never been able to get Mehran into a costume, and I've been trying since we were fifteen. As far as Mehran is concerned, Halloween is the one day of the year when he has a valid excuse to wear black eyeliner. That's his "costume." Black eyeliner. He's so psyched. I knew Bill and Scout wouldn't come in costume, but I hoped they'd at least suit up in the bacon and eggs costumes I provided. And they did. They kept the costumes on for a whole thirty minutes. I was impressed. Gueran promised that he'd wear some fabulous costume showcasing his impressive package, but he came through the door carrying said costume in a tied-up plastic grocery bag and left with it in the same bag, unworn.

Our doorbell was starting to ring. Oh boy! It was time. Jack and his buddies asked if they could man the candy distribution, and our motley group of many grown-ups and a few token kids headed out to trick-or-treat. I'd wanted a house with a kid-friendly neighborhood, and now I had it in spades. We opened the door to madness. Couldn't you have guessed? Beaver Avenue was Halloween Central. Another neighborhood perk. The block was churning with screaming kids in every costume known to man, sprinting from decked-out house to decked-out house. It looked like the L.A. riots had returned, except this time the rioters were all three feet tall and dressed as Power Rangers. Girls were stopping Cinderella (Jenny) for her autograph. Candy and abandoned costume accessories were scattered on the ground. The street was as crowded as an amusement park on a Saturday. It was crazy. Liam had no idea what was going on. Dean carried him to the house next door, knocked on the door, and said, "Trick or treat!" Our neighbor handed Liam some malt balls. Aha! A light went on. Liam squirmed out of Dean's arms and tore off down the block without us, a fearless little bee darting in and out of houses asking for candy. But he was only one and a half. He couldn't focus on his mission—or anything—for very long. Soon enough he got distracted by the pretty lights and the candy was forgotten.

About half an hour later we hurried home to help out Jack with the trick-or-treaters, who were marching from house to house like ants at a picnic. Back inside, Liam held out a lollipop to me to unwrap. Without thinking, I opened it up and handed it back to him. Sara's daughter, Emma, stared at me with wide eyes and immediately turned to her mother, saying, "I want a lollipop too!" Sara shot me a look that said, "She's never had a lollipop before, but now I kind of have to give her one." Oops. Emma wanted her first lollipop, and it was my fault. It hadn't even occurred to me to be careful of what the other kids would want, much less to withhold Liam's lollipop. Believe me, when it came to lollipops, this wasn't Liam's first day at the races. I apologized to Sara and thought, *Great, I'm that mom*. The one who didn't think twice about feeding her small child sugar on a stick and corrupted her friend's child.

I had never handed people candy before, but I threw myself into the front door job. Holding out the big bowl of Snickers, M&M's, 3 Musketeers, et cetera, I said, "Go ahead! Take two or three! Take more!" "Take more" had an unexpected effect on the children. They plunged elbow deep into the bowl and scooped an armload into their bags. I looked down at the bowl. Whoa. It was half gone. But I couldn't help myself. I wanted to be that house, the one the kids whisper about as they pass one another on the sidewalk. No wonder we ran out of candy so many times.

Dean kept going back to the corner drugstore until they closed. I didn't want to turn away trick-or-treaters! I was in the kitchen trying desperately to whip up some cupcakes when Mehran came in and said, "Lisa Macey is at the door." He was joking. He *had* to be joking. Lisa was my friend in high school, but we were friends like Shannen Doherty and I were friends.

That is to say, she was the alpha female and I was her little side-kick, doing whatever she told me to do.

Lisa once dictated how I should dress, and her idea of fashion was oversized men's sweatshirts, Doc Martens, and unbrushed hair thrown up on top of her head. She made me listen to rap; she was all into NWA. I hated rap! But I listened to it anyway. I may have been the only person in the world who listened to gangsta rap because I'd been told to. Lisa was the friend who'd say, "Let's get in your car, drive down the block to the park outside your parents', drink Bartles & Jaymes wine coolers, and smoke cigarettes." She made me feel like I had to smoke if I wanted to be in the cool group. Worst of all, she made me smoke Marlboro Reds.

Once Lisa was running down the hall of our house. Nanny told her to stop, and Lisa ignored her. When Nanny told her to be respectful, Lisa said, "You can't tell me what to do." To Nanny! I never talked back to Nanny. And from the look on Nanny's face when she told me about this encounter, I know there was more to it than that. Whatever Lisa said or did, after that day Nanny stated that she wasn't allowed in our house anymore. Period. End of discussion.

Why was I friends with someone who bossed me around and didn't let me be myself? I guess Lisa was the precursor to the bad-boy boyfriends I would have until I met my first husband. She made fun of people. She was big and kind of scary. There was no reason I should have been with her. And now Mehran was claiming that she was at my door.

There was one good thing about Lisa Macey. She introduced me to all my best friends. She went to my all-girls school but she lived in the Valley. Through her I met Jenny, Jennifer, Kevin, and Mehran, the people who are still my best friends today. As soon as high school ended we all stopped being friends with her—her reign of terror was over; we were free—but over the years she became our personal urban legend. Mehran would always be like, "Oh my God, Lisa Macey's here," to freak me out. So when I was in the kitchen trying to make cupcakes for the masses of trick-or-treaters and he said, "Lisa Macey's at your door! She wants to say hi." I was like, "Ha. Ha."

Mehran said, "No, I swear to God." Still skeptical, waiting for him to shout, "Halloween Fools!" or whatever, I went into the front hall, and there she was. She was thin, pretty, and dressed like a girl. Actually, she was dressed like a witch, but a hip witch in all black with a cool leather jacket and a witch's hat. She smiled sweetly. A few cute kids standing politely at her side said, "Trick or treat!" This was a girl who in high school thought everything was bullshit and was always outside smoking. Now she was a lovely woman whose sister's family lived a block away. She said, "I have car seats in my car now," and we laughed. Here was Lisa Macey, who'd been so scary and different, whom we'd built into a nemesis. Now she was perfectly normal and nice. It was one of those moments that makes all the drama and angst of youth permanently dissolve into harmless memories. As she walked away she said, "Facebook me."

I looked around me at my half-costumed friends and out at the street, still a pleasant stream of sugar-addled kids. Whatever different struggles Lisa and I had gone through as kids, we'd come through. We'd found what we wanted and needed, and settled down to the lives we chose. I felt joyful and calm at the same time. This was it, the Halloween I'd dreamed of.

After Lisa left, Halloween felt over. My cupcakes never quite happened, it was 9:30, and we had nothing left to offer. Besides, most of the trick-or-treaters at this point were either clearly on their second lap or over six feet tall, dressed in T-shirts, and plainly too old for trick-or-treating. We admitted defeat and shut off the lights. Liam and Stella were long asleep. Our friends took their sleepy, sugared-out kids home, and I went upstairs to begin the long process of extracting myself from my bee costume. As I undressed, Dean made some comment about how stripper bee wasn't such a ridiculous idea after all. I took one last look in the mirror at the yellow and black false eyelashes and winked at myself. Those eyelashes were too good.

elizabethmessina.com

My Little Monkey's
First Birthday Party

Okay, I get it—perhaps
slightly terrifying to a
twelve-month-old.

elizabethmessina.com

Confirmed! Completely terrifying.
Note to self: small cake sans
jungle animals next year.

All the bells and whistles and Liam is
happiest with the decorative bananas.
Didn't I learn anything from my
childhood?

elizabethmessina.com

Red Cheese

The McDermotts SAY CHEESE!

My homemade red velvet cake for the block party . . . moments before it came crashing down!

Liam and wagon all decorated to fit in at the Beaver Avenue Fourth of July block party.

Do we fit in? Me and the Guncles lawning it
to watch Fourth of July festivities.

My Suburban Dream?!

Just another day for Liam in L.A.: sunshine, cameras, and lounging in an inflatable duckie.

Liam Lovefest

My little man learns to walk and I learn to balance the beach ball . . . er, belly that's about to pop!

Mommy and her boy enjoy a swim . . . pre-pool-poo incident.

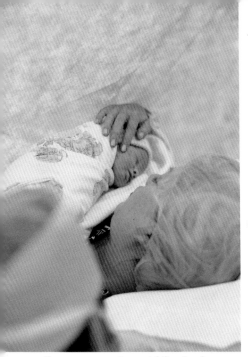

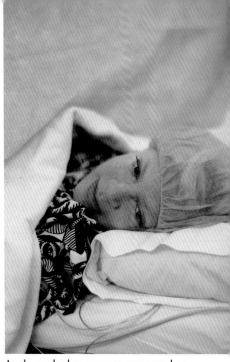

I meet my precious girl for the first time. She's so beautiful!

As they take her away to measure her, overwhelming fear hits me that I no longer can completely protect her.

A Stella Is Born!

I have my loving husband, little boy, and now baby girl . . . complete bliss.

Mimi La Rue—
a True Star

Mimi, the protector.

elizabethmessina.com

Mimi always knew
her good angle!

Malibu Mimi—
bikini ready.

Stella Shines

Stella's first head shot . . . that's a joke, by the way!

Subliminal message: Don't worry, Mommy. You and I are going to have a very special mother/daughter bond.

Hours after giving birth to Stella . . . It's just another day in Mommywood as I sign my book *sTORI telling* for a nurse.

The BEE Family.

Halloween '08

My little Ladybug proudly dons her
kinda-made-by-mama costume.

The family that dresses up together, stays together.

Liam riding the sugar high.

Perhaps the next
Michael Phelps?

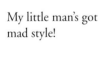

My little man's got
mad style!

The Guncles partake in Liam's fave hobby—swimming.

My besties—Jenny and Mehran.

Don't all moms garden and drink champagne with their baby nurses?

elizabethmessina.com

Liam processes the existence of his new sister Stella.

Stella and Liam wait for the Great Pumpkin.

Liam and Stella with their big brother, Jack.

Dean's an amazing daddy.
My proudest shot.

m home. Perfect—it didn't really matter where we went first, long as we were all together as a family.

We were taking the two babies and Patsy, which meant a two-bedroom suite, so I emailed a couple of publicists to find out if I could get a good rate. Yes, I confess I dropped my own name, hoping that would get me a discount. I'm not proud. There are some minuses to living a very public life; this was one of the pluses. Almost immediately after I sent the email out, I got a response from one of the publicists. She said that we could have a completely free vacation at a nice-looking resort in the desert if we posed for one family picture and did an interview with *OK!* magazine. The poolside photo—the one you see in magazines—that's how it sometimes comes about. Seems like a no-brainer, right? You definitely couldn't beat that rate. (Well, I guess *they* could pay *us,* but let's not go overboard here.) But this was our first family vacation. Exposing my life to the press is part of how I make a living, but I have to draw the line with my family somewhere. All I wanted was a true getaway. And a discount if possible. I wrote back saying thanks anyway but that we were happy to pay. This was a family trip and we really didn't want to do any publicity.

On the Friday that our vacation was to begin, Dean had some phone interviews to do, so I left him at home and headed out with the children and Patsy. After about half an hour on the freeway, Patsy and I realized that a little black car was following us. A paparazzo. Definitely one of the minuses of celebrity life.

elizabethmessina.com

Daddy's Biker Boy!

There's a tree with shiny lights, tons of baked goods, and a man named Santa brings me gifts? I could get used to this holiday—even if Mom makes us wear matching jammies.

elizabethmessina.com

My beautiful family.

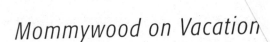

Mommywood on Vacation

Halloween felt like one of those milestones I'd always imagined when I pictured being a mother, and another one was on the horizon. It was time for us to take our first vacation as a family of four, minus cameras. The photo that you'd see in a magazine would be me, Dean, Liam, and tiny Stella relaxing poolside. But nothing's as simple as it looks in magazines. There are perks and drawbacks to being famous, and they all came to play on our trip.

When Stella was born, Dean and I went back to work without a break, so by the time the end of the show's season rolled around, we were dying for a vacation. At first I thought we'd go someplace far away and exotic. We initially considered Maui, but that seemed a little too ambitious. Then we talked about Cabo, a much shorter flight, but Stella seemed too young to go to Mexico. Finally we settled on the desert. A two-hour drive

If I slowed down, he slowed down. If I sped up, he sped up. If I switched lanes, he switched lanes. It's creepy being chased like that. The natural impulse is to try to get away. I pulled off on the left shoulder and waited there with my hazards on. I thought he'd zoom by, but he pulled over too. I tried various lane-changing tricks and maneuvers, but every time I looked in the rearview mirror, there he was, my unwelcome companion. This went on for a good hour, and then I saw it. My opportunity for escape. I was in the carpool lane on the far left. A big truck was driving along in the lane next to me. I sped up, pulled out in front of the truck, zoomed across all four lanes of the highway, and screeched off the first exit ramp I saw. Patsy didn't say anything, but out of the corner of my eye I saw her braced against the dashboard for dear life. It was not exactly the safe driving I wanted to model for my young children, but I saw no other way to shake him. And honestly I don't know what's less safe—driving aggressively for a moment or allowing a persistent stranger to track us all the way to our destination.

When I caught my breath I looked around and saw that we had exited in West Covina. Patsy took a deep breath and wiped her brow, but my adrenaline was still pumping. I was sure that the paparazzo had taken the next exit (East Covina? Central Covina?) and was speeding back to West Covina to hunt us down. It was a sketchy neighborhood (well, sketchy by my admittedly warped standards), so I pulled into the parking lot of the first wholesome place I saw—a school—to hide from our pursuer. Hiding there in our Range Rover. Because there were so many other Range Rovers in the West Covina school parking lot. Very subtle.

Stella started screaming. When she started, Liam joined in. Worst singing duo ever. At first I thought Stella was rightfully protesting my driving technique, but when I checked on her I saw that she had a huge poop. A major poop. I'm talking poop up the puss. I swear it was all the way up to her belly button. I know I always wanted a baby girl, and I was beyond thrilled to have Stella. But one incontestable benefit to the boy baby is that there is no such thing as poop up the puss. Patsy comforted Liam while I changed Stella's diaper in the front seat of the car. It was a hundred degrees out. We'd been in the West Covina parking lot for half an hour. I texted Dean, "We're hiding from a paparazzo in some random neighborhood and Stella has poop up the puss." Well, I used the standard texting abbreviations, like PUTP.

At last the coast—and the poop—were clear. The children were calm again and we got back on the road and made our way to the resort. Upon our arrival we found that we'd been upgraded to the presidential suite. Awesome! Instead of the small split room we'd booked for us and the single for Patsy, we now were the lucky residents of an enormous three-bedroom suite, with a private pool, a Jacuzzi, and its own garage. It felt like a trade-off for the paparazzo: he was the burden that came with who I was, and the upgrade was the benefit.

Liam loves hotels. As soon as we walk into a hotel room he does a little happy hotel dance. When I was a child I always liked small, cozy places, but when Liam burst into that huge suite, he was psyched. He was especially fascinated with the bedposts. He'd never seen bedposts before. He stared at them for a good thirty minutes while we unloaded the car and fed Stella.

Dean eventually arrived. A little room service, a movie or two on the DVD player, and we all settled down for our first night of vacation. There were a few cockroaches on the sink, but we trapped them under glasses and didn't worry about them. We were in the presidential suite. I'm sure they were the classiest cockroaches the resort had to offer. We weren't about to complain.

Who traps cockroaches but doesn't kill them? I'd never dealt with cockroaches before. It was our first night in a new place. Killing them seemed like a bad omen. I wouldn't let Dean do it. Of course, the next day the cockroaches had escaped. I just hoped they would go home to their friends and relations, tell the tale of their night of horror, and stage an exodus, far from the glass cages of the presidential suite. Anyway, that morning Dean and I had more important things to worry about. We were on a mission: Target. We needed a few critical items. You know, food and beverages for the fridge. Diapers. Movies. Toys for Liam. Toys for Stella. Pool toys for Liam. A portable swing for Stella. A ride-on truck for Liam. More food and beverages. Elaborate floating devices that could save us all in case of a hurricane. We spent a solid two hours stocking up at Target. By the time we were done we could have moved to the desert.

For a while we saw no need to leave our presidential suite. You know how the president just stays at the White House or Camp David and doesn't go out much because everything's there already? It was like that. There was room service. There were TVs. A full-sized pool. Beds. And a bomb shelter's worth of supplies from Target. The first few days flew by. I had an okay massage. We rented bikes—Dean's had a little seat for Liam up front—and rode around the resort while Patsy and Stella followed behind in a golf cart.

Eating at the restaurants wasn't such a big success. Liam was always an easy baby. Patsy says she's never had a baby as good—not even her own kids. He loved being out. He rarely cried. He never sent food back to the kitchen. We'd be in Europe at a fancy restaurant at ten at night after a long flight, and Liam would be there, chilling in his baby carrier. Airplane trips, crowds, flashing lights? No problem. Liam was always game to hang out and take it all in. Stella? Not so chill. She doesn't want to be held or rocked sitting down. No, sir. Princess Stella would like you to walk. Maybe it's because I was so crazy busy when I was pregnant. She got used to constant movement. Whatever the reason, you can't just sit at dinner holding her. Princess Stella must be carried around, and as soon as you try to sit down, she wakes up and starts screaming. Her face turns bright red and her little legs go all rigid.

The one night we tried to eat at one of the restaurants, Liam got obsessed with the Bavarian music at another restaurant downstairs and refused to stay put. Dean ordered some food to go and the two of them went off to hear the music. I stayed back, thinking maybe Stella and I could have a mother-daughter dinner, but I ended up walking Stella around the restaurant instead of eating or feeding her. That was when I first realized that having children at dinner is the best diet plan I know.

The next morning I had a moment of fear when Dean put Liam in the hot tub. I was pretty sure kids under ten or twelve or twenty or something weren't supposed to go in hot tubs. Liam usually splashes around in the pool, but in the hot tub he sat on the top step, looking spaced out and mellow. I was trying to be cool, but finally I couldn't take it anymore. What was the hot tub doing to my little boy? I said to Dean, "How do we know that his insides aren't cooking?" Dean said, "He's just relaxing." But Liam was so dopey, I thought maybe his system had already started shutting down. I was certain we were making Liam soup. I said, "Liam! Liam! Look at Mama," and prodded him gently, but he didn't respond. I knew it! Organ failure! I swept him out of the hot tub. Liam immediately came to life and started screaming, "Water, water!" He flailed and struggled to get back in the tub. When I put him back in the hot water, he instantly relaxed again. The kid has a stressful life; should have known he needed his spa time.

Liam is a water baby. So long as we were in the pool, he was happy. But eventually we thought it would be nice for him to have contact with other children out in the general pool.

It was a hot, sunny desert day. The main pool wasn't too

crowded, just a nice bunch of families, with kids jumping around between the big pool and the kiddie pool. Some parents were relaxing, some were in the water with their kids. If there were child-free people at the resort, they were definitely segregating themselves from the Marco Polo culture of the main pool.

Dean and I wrangled a couple of lounge chairs and got settled. In a matter of seconds everyone was staring at us. Now, people don't react the way you think they might in these situations. It's not like they glance over, notice who we are, watch for a bit, shrug their shoulders and go "huh" in a vaguely anticlimactic way, then go back to their lives. No, they stare at us, stare some more, take a sip of a beverage without breaking eye contact, and then just keep staring. Sometimes when we're at a restaurant, people will walk up to the table and stand there staring at me like I'm an animal in a zoo. They don't say a word, they just stand there with mouths open, hands on hips. It's always funny to me. It reminds me of the moment in *Mary Poppins* when, after Julie Andrews does some sort of magic or another, she tells the boy, "Close your mouth, Michael, we are not a codfish." Dean often says, "Yes, it's her," just to break the silence. I guess I'm used to it because it's been happening for as long as I can remember, but in a way I'm also not used to it, because no matter how often it occurs, being stared at makes me uncomfortable. I think that would be true for anybody.

At the pool, nobody walked right up to me to stare. Instead, out of nowhere, the cameras appeared. Suddenly everyone was taking family photos at the pool! They'd snap a few token shots, then send their kids to stand strategically in front of us so they could pretend to take photos of them while really snapping us. Using the kids, always in good taste. (This is another way those poolside photos come about—sold to magazines by any Joe with a cell phone camera and a hungry wallet.)

Patsy always reminds us to be gracious to the people who can't help staring; she says these people are our biggest supporters. They're our fans. And I get what it's like to see someone in real life when you already feel like you know them from the screen. I get starstruck too. Once I saw Jerry Springer and asked him to take a picture with me. And when Erin Moran hugged me with unforeseen exuberance at the Sixty-second Annual Mother Goose Parade, I was secretly thinking, "Wow, Joanie Cunningham just accidentally brushed up against my boob." Starstruck, yes. But I can't say I ever stand in front of celebrities and stare at them as if they're not real. It's staring! It just feels odd.

Dean took Liam into the pool, and the woman in a flowery caftan next to me caught my eye. "They're so cute," she said. I thanked her and smiled. She pointed at Stella. "What's her name?" When I told her, she said, "Oh, that's right." She looked over at the pool and said, "And he's Liam." Then she gave me a conspiratorial wink and said, "Don't worry. I'm not going to tell anyone." Everyone else was already staring at us. I loved that she was whispering like we were sharing a big secret. Thanks a lot, flowery caftan woman.

I escaped into the kiddie pool with Liam, and Dean took Stella in the big pool for the first time. She loved it. But she was only four months old. The doctor said they're not supposed to swim until six months. This was worse than Liam in the hot tub. I knew for certain that we were violating the doctor's orders. What was wrong with the pool? What was it going to do to her? Didn't they basically spend their first nine months in the equivalent of a very small heated pool? It was all about fertility, wasn't it? It always was. The hormones in milk would bring on early-onset puberty. The wrong baby bottles would destroy their fertility. Probably at that very moment the chlorine was making its way up her vagina and destroying my chances of ever having grandchildren. But before I could get even more paranoid, I noticed something floating near Liam. At first I thought it was a dead leaf. I went to scoop it away from him, but the moment it was in my hand, a horrible realization dawned on me. I wasn't holding a dead leaf. I was holding a piece of poo. Now this was a photo op I prayed nobody would exploit.

Liam's poops in the pool were like a ritual. By now I knew how to manage the poopy swim diaper. But this was a whole new ball of wax. (Except I would have been a lot happier to deal with wax.) I had never experienced this before. The poop was not *contained*. The water around Liam was starting to get murky. The whole pool was a hot zone. Children were splashing around, blowing bubbles, oblivious. Moms and dads were smiling and laughing. And cameras, everywhere! Everything seemed to be moving in Technicolor slow motion. Any minute those happy faces would darken with realization. There was no other option. I had to get out of there—and fast. I grabbed Liam, signaled Dean (you know, that universal husband-wife sign language for "our kid just shit in the pool and we are out of here"), and just fled. Yes, I made Dean call in the incident once we got back to the room. I don't know what subsequent action was taken. I can't make any guarantees. But that, parents, is why you should never, ever go in the kiddie pool.

After our pool adventure, we stayed in retreat. Then, a few days later, Liam woke up in the middle of the night crying. We brought him into bed with us, but he kept sitting up and moaning, "Home, home." He had bed head. It was cute, but he was not a happy camper. And finally he moaned, "Home, home, home, goddammit." I wanted to laugh so hard; I don't know where he'd picked that up. But it got his point across: Liam was done with vacation.

We all slept in after a long night. In the morning Liam was in bed, watching cartoons, when he sat on Stella's head. That was it. We were done.

In spite of his meltdown, Liam was a pro, comfortable on planes and in new spaces. I wanted Stella to see the world too, so as they grew up we could all have adventures as a family. The whole first year of Liam's life we traveled constantly, for work and for fun. We went to Europe on business when he was two months old. By four months he had been in London, Scotland, Toronto, and New York.

My father swore off planes at the age of eighteen when he narrowly avoided traveling on a plane that crashed with no survivors. Consequently, my parents never took us anywhere requiring a plane trip. By the time I could travel and had the means to do so, I was terrified of flying. I got homesick when I stayed in hotels. It's hard to break out of what you grow up thinking is normal. I always tell Dean that it's important to me that we see the world with our children.

I know that someday Dean and I will take vacations alone, but I really want the children to grow up traveling the world, seeing and learning things. We've worked hard. If we can afford to take our children, I want to do that and not keep all the adventures to ourselves. I want them to feel safe and comfortable. I don't want my fear of flying to be passed down to another generation. But mostly I just want the kids with us. I want to stare at Liam and Stella constantly. They're so amazing to me. The desert was the beginning of something. Baby steps.

Stepmommywood

The whole time we were in the desert there was drama about my stepson Jack's tenth birthday party. A week before Jack's party he decided that he didn't want me to come.

I went into my relationship with Dean knowing that the man I fell in love with had a child already. It was part of the deal, and it sounded great to me. I loved the man. I loved his child too. The two feelings were inseparable. When I first met and fell in love with Dean in Ottawa, before I even knew what would happen when we went home to L.A. or whether we'd find a way to be together, I started carrying around a picture of Jack. I thought of Jack as my new son. Not in a possessive or competitive way. I wasn't planning to be his mother. I was just gung ho. I wasn't worrying about the details. In that lovefest moment I didn't think through how the relationship would actually work. I'd never had a baby, much less a child. How could I begin to imagine what it would be like to have a step-child? And then to have babies?

When Dean and I first met, he and his family lived in L.A. For the first year that Dean and I were together, Jack spent every other weekend with us, as well as every other Tuesday and Thursday night. After Dean and Mary Jo settled their divorce, she moved her family to Canada. Then we saw Jack less often. He came for long holidays—for Christmas, for a month during the summer. It was hard for Dean to see him less often, but the three of us had a great time on those visits. Dean and I were in our fun, honeymoon phase and we made each day of Jack's visits special, going to play baseball, going to Chuck E. Cheese, and so on. I felt like I was reliving my childhood. Actually, this was a whole new world to me. I was living the childhood I wished I'd had.

Then, soon after Stella was born, Mary Jo decided to move back to Los Angeles. She told Dean that she wanted Jack to be near him. This meant Jack's time was split much more evenly between his two parents. Now Jack was moving back and forth from her house to our house every week. When he was visiting I had three children to take care of. I want to be careful here. I love Jack, and I don't want to write anything that will ever hurt him. What I want to talk about is how in a family with chil-dren from different marriages, there are times when everyone has to shift gears.

When you have a baby, you start at the beginning. You watch a child grow. You have a history together. When you suddenly have a ten-year-old living with you, you're starting midstream. He's already half-formed. He has a history without you. There are traditions and rules and behaviors in place and you're just jumping into the middle of his life. It's pretty mind-blowing. No matter how much Dean and I talked about Jack, it was impossible for me to feel prepared. And I'm sure Jack felt the same way. We had to stumble and feel our way toward a relationship that worked for us, one that can't have been easy for him in the first place. It's a constant, ongoing effort to find the balance between being a mother figure to him and not overstepping the bounds of a stepmom. Kids need boundaries to function, but how am I supposed to know what those boundaries are? I'm raising infants!

Here's another challenge: should Jack live by the rules of our household, or should we follow the rules of his mother's household? Family dinners have always been important to me. In my mind, at dinnertime everyone is given the same nutritious meal—say turkey meatloaf, broccoli, and mashed potatoes—and everyone eats what they want of that meal. But Jack's mother might believe in giving him choices. Or she might believe in the Clean Plate Club. Or she might want him to be a vegetarian. So he sits down to a table with one set of ideas, whatever they are, and is expected to abide by another. It's tough to know how and what lines to draw. I wanted to be a good parent-figure while not intruding on his birth parents.

In theory, I should look to Dean, as Jack's dad, to draw those lines. But Dean still feels guilty about the divorce, while I can be emotionally removed. I think sometimes Dean's too lenient with Jack. Meanwhile, Dean says I'm quick to reinforce rules with Jack but that Liam needs boundaries as well. When it comes down to it, I actually think the hardest part isn't being a stepmom. It's caring for kids who are so far apart in age.

Jack didn't want me to come to his birthday party—he's a kid, he's still dealing with mixed feelings about me—but we thought it was best for me to be a constant, positive presence in his life. At first we came up with an alternate plan. Instead of my coming to his party, we would have a family dinner: me, Dean, Mary Jo, Jack, and two of his friends. The only time I'd ever met Mary Jo was when I went to her house because she wanted to discuss how we cared for Jack. I became so paranoid that she had it in for me that I had a kitchen knife hidden in my purse in case I needed it for self-defense. I was honest, maybe too honest, about that encounter when I wrote about it in *sTORI telling*. Mary Jo never said anything about my book. Jack never said anything either, until one day he said, "Everyone says Tori wrote this book trashing her whole family." Dean said, "Did you read the book?" Jack said, "No." Dean said, "Well then, you can't judge."

It's a no-brainer that I would never say anything negative about Mary Jo in front of Jack. But when Jack said to me, "My mom says you're the ugliest living thing in this world," I had a feeling Mary Jo and I didn't read the same rule book. (Er, I'm pretty sure her rule book says something about it being very uncool to fall in love with other women's husbands.) I just said,

"Yeah, that's not very nice to say about people. But I think your mom's very pretty and you can tell her I said that."

This family dinner would be the first time I'd seen Mary Jo since the knife-in-my-purse encounter. It would be the first time I'd ever seen Mary Jo with Dean and Jack. It would be the first time we all tried to be a big, integrated, crazy modern-day family.

We went to Miceli's, an Italian restaurant in the Valley famous for its singing waiters. When we walked in, I gave Mary Jo the warmest "Hi" you've ever heard, being sure to make eye contact. I wanted to set a friendly tone. We all walked to the booth. Mary Jo sat down, and then I slid in right next to her. I didn't want to wait a beat. I figured, if I just pretended we were all friends, out to have a nice, celebratory dinner, it would kind of be true. Mary Jo was fine. She was perfectly nice. If the way we acted in each other's company that evening was the way we acted in our separate homes, I was sure Jack would have a seamless transition into a split, but warm and loving, family.

And yet. Even though to all appearances it was a normal dinner, I somehow felt inferior to Mary Jo. I have no idea why. She was so proper and mature. When I giggled I felt like a silly schoolgirl. When we got our food, I looked down to make sure I had my utensils in the right order. I felt twelve. It was nothing she did or said to me, and granted, it was an uncomfortable situation all around. For some reason I just felt like I wasn't smart enough or cultured enough. Later, when I told Dean, he just said, "Welcome to my world."

But we all had to admit that the dinner went smoothly. Our family was nothing Jack had to be embarrassed about. There would be no drama if I came to his birthday party. So we decided that I would go after all. It was a laser tag party at a space in the Valley. I was nervous about what my role was and how Mary Jo would treat me, but as it turned out, it wasn't Dean's ex-wife whose behavior would surprise me, it was my ex-costar.

The first thing that happened at the party was that everyone gathered in a briefing room to learn how to play laser tag. There were about twenty people there. I already knew that at Jack's new school he had befriended another boy whose name was Jack too. One day when Dean went to pick Jack up from school, he met the other Jack and realized that it was Jack Perry, son of my former costar Luke Perry.

We knew Jack Perry was coming to the birthday party, and when I entered the briefing room I saw Dean sitting with Liam in his lap, a space next to him, and then Luke. It had been a while, and I was happy to see Luke. In fact, I figured he probably came to the party in part because he thought I was going to be there. I squeezed into the place between Luke and Dean, said, "Hi!" and leaned in to give him a kiss and a hug. He sat there. Stone.

I pulled back. Luke stared straight ahead at the woman giving the laser tag lecture. I sat there in the seat right next to him, half listening to the instructions (even though I didn't plan to play) and half completely puzzled. I tried to work out why he'd given me the cold shoulder. Maybe he was busy trying to focus on how to play laser tag. No, now he was checking his BlackBerry. Maybe he thought we'd catch up later? But when the woman finished, he slipped out of the briefing room without saying a word to me. I was completely mystified. And uncomfortable. As if this birthday party hadn't been awkward enough to begin with.

My friend Scout was sitting next to Mary Jo for the instructional section. When it was over, she turned to him and said, "Are you playing?"

Scout said, "No."

She said, "Can you hold my purse?" and handed it to Scout. Then Mary Jo went off with the kids to play laser tag, and Scout came out of the room holding Mary Jo's purse, bewildered.

I took Liam into the arcade room to see all the flashing lights. Luke continued to ignore me. When we crossed paths, he walked right by me as if I were a wall. At one point he came up to me and Dean and started to talk to Dean. I figured I'd been imagining things, that he was there to talk to me and Dean together, but when I turned to him, he walked away. At one point I came out of the arcade room holding Liam and saw Luke looking my way. I made sure I caught his eye. Ha! He'd have to say something to me now. And indeed he did. He said, "Where's the bathroom?" in an angry tone. Maybe the laser tag pizza didn't agree with him. I said, "I don't know," then suddenly felt guilty about not knowing the layout of the laser tag facility. He rolled his eyes and walked away.

My friend Scout was with me at the party for moral support. I told him what was going on and he said, "It's gotta be the book." I racked my brain. What had I written in my book that made Luke hate me? I couldn't think of anything. Finally Scout said, "The Christmas party. You wrote about him punching out Nick at your parents' Christmas party." It was true. I had written about Luke fighting with my then boyfriend. But in that story Luke was my friend and hero. He was protecting me from a bad boyfriend. I admired him and was grateful to him for that act.

If the problem was that Luke wasn't wild about my book, well, he wouldn't be the only former costar to have a less-than-thrilled reaction. Ian Ziering did some interviews saying he was upset about my book, that I blew things out of proportion. He said I shouldn't have spoken badly about the experience. Of course the news magazines ran his comments as if we were in a huge blowout: "Ian vs. Tori." But the next time I saw Ian was at the Silver Spoon Dog and Baby Buffet, which is basically a celebrity free-gifts party, in Century City. I was extremely pregnant with Stella, and Dean and I were being interviewed by *Access Hollywood*. Out of nowhere, Ian appeared and jumped into our shot, all smiles, patting my pregnant belly and saying, "Hi, Mama."

As for Shannen Doherty, she was on the cover of *Us Weekly* with the headline Shannen "Defends Herself Against Tori Spelling's 'Lies.'" I got emails from friends and fans saying, "Oh my God, I can't believe she said that," but I wasn't concerned. I know I told the truth as I saw it, and she probably felt that she was doing the same. Regardless, I'm pretty sure that her accusations caused a spike in the sales of my book.

When I thought about it more, I decided that if I knew Luke, he hadn't read the book at all. What happened is that he probably got questioned about it by friends and the media. They'd say something like, "Tori wrote that you punched out her boyfriend at her parents' house." Maybe they made it sound like a bad thing. Or maybe he just didn't like having those years rehashed at all. Did all that brooding as Dylan McKay rub off on him?

I know, I know. In an ideal world I would have simply walked up to him and asked him what was wrong. But he was *so* cold. So instead, I hid. Seriously, at some point I really have to learn to confront people because the mystery of that behavior will just eat at me. By the end of the party I was like, *Wow, compared to Luke, Mary Jo's a breath of fresh air.*

I have to admit that I was surprised, pretty much across the board, by the way people reacted to my book. With a few exceptions—notably my mother and a couple of things I said about Shannen (and even then I tried to see both sides of the stories)—I really tried to save the worst, most embarrassing revelations for myself. I tried to be aware of everyone else's feelings and privacy, and I'm sorry if some of the stories I thought were positive (like Luke's punch-out) or funny at my expense (like bringing a knife in my purse when I met Mary Jo for the first time) were not thought so by other people.

I live a public life, and when other people cross into that life, I have to weigh my rights to be public against their rights to be private. If celebrities, who are used to the attention and the way the media warps its presentation of facts, reacted so strongly to what I thought were tiny, innocuous mentions, then how must Mary Jo have felt? The discomfort I felt at Miceli's must have been minor next to the discomfort Mary Jo experienced from knowing people had read personal things about my relationship with the man who was now her ex-husband.

There is more to say about being a stepmother, but it's not my right to say more, not if I care about the people involved, and I do very much. That's a lesson I've learned the hard way from my last book.

Retail and Therapy

We were a family of five now, and we needed to work on the issues that arose from Jack's moving back to town and Liam's being so attached to Dean. I grew up in a situation where I didn't have to take care of myself, much less take care of others. People did everything for me. Now I realized that Dean was doing the same—doing most of the heavy lifting while I stood by as helpless as when I was a girl whose parents had a household staff of at least twelve. I didn't want to be that helpless person anymore—especially if it interfered with my relationship with my children—but I didn't know how to be anyone else. How do you transform a Hollywood starlet into the responsible, confident wife and mother she has always wanted to be? A little couples therapy was in order. Dean and I went back to see Dr. Wexler, the therapist who had guided me through the end of my first marriage.

I hadn't seen Dr. Wexler for years, but I knew that she did family counseling. So we went in there and described the situation. I had to admit that when I found out I was having a girl, part of me was excited because she was bound to do girl things—things that Dean hadn't experienced with his boys already. I love that Dean and Liam have such a close relationship, and most of the time I know that Liam loves me like crazy, but I hoped to have more of that "new parents together" experience with Dean and Stella. I also talked about how I felt that Dean didn't let me do enough—that I wanted to participate but when I did he sometimes criticized me.

When Dean's turn came, he said that I was overthinking it, that parenting was instinct. He didn't want to have to think about who was doing what and whether things were shaking out evenly. He thought I should just step in and do it. What was he supposed to do if he came in and saw that Liam had a dirty diaper? Let Liam get a diaper rash while everyone waited for me to notice?

As we described the situation, Dr. Wexler said that our dynamic was pretty common but that she usually heard it in reverse. The wife usually complained about the husband's not doing enough, and the husband usually said that she didn't give him a chance. The husband would say that when he did try to step in, the wife told him he wasn't doing the job right. Instead, in our case, Dean was the experienced dad, and it was all new to me. I needed some freedom to make mistakes and learn from them.

Instead of helping out with the everyday work of parenting, I overcompensated in the ways I knew how to show my love. Liam always started to cry whenever Dean and I had to go to a meeting. (And let's face it, he was probably crying because *Daddy* was leaving.) Dean always made a quick exit. He said, "Bye, buddy, see you later," and he was out. But I always took much longer, rubbing Liam's head and explaining to him, "It's okay, Monkey. We'll be back. We always come back." Dean always got annoyed with me for taking too long. He said you needed to treat leaving like ripping off a Band-Aid. Just say you'll be back and quickly walk away. No matter how many times he told me this, I couldn't bring myself to make a quick departure. It drove Dean nuts. Dr. Wexler told Dean that in theory he was right, sure, but he couldn't control the way I felt. Because I'm not the primary caregiving parent in our minds, I felt a need to grow my bond with Liam, so I doted more on him. Maybe it was more for my benefit than Liam's, but that didn't mean it was all bad.

Dean and I both work, and we work together, so on paper our parenting is pretty equal. It's been that way from the beginning, and I love that. But it surprised me how quickly our own childhoods and Dean's experience as a dad came into play in the dynamics we developed. I wanted to make sure the decisions we made as parents were shared and deliberate and as free from our own baggage as possible. Going into couples therapy gave us insight almost immediately.

One inspiring session of therapy later, I decided that the best way to build my independent bonds with my children was to spend time with them alone. I decided to take Stella on her first shopping excursion. Neil Lane, the famous jewelry designer, was having a party to celebrate the opening of his store, and I had to find a dress for the event, then go to Neil Lane to pick out the jewelry I would wear with the dress.

Stella was four months old. I know it sounds crazy, but it was really the first time Stella and I went out alone! Dean and I go everywhere together. But now that Jack was in town, Dean had independent obligations; some days he was picking up Jack from school or taking Jack to karate. It was about time that I started to do more by myself.

We pulled up to Neiman Marcus. Stella was cooing in her infant car seat, an Orbit, which is the celebrity-choice car seat, because it has 360-degree rotation, some new high-tech foam, and a sunshade that the Orbit website actually calls a paparazzi shield! I like to think that they used that phrase after watching *Tori & Dean,* since as far as I could tell, it showed up on their website after I called it that on the show. Anyway, I planned to snap the car seat into its stroller base, but when I opened the trunk, the base wasn't there. The base is always there. Dean always puts it back after he uses it. But this time it wasn't there, and I hadn't thought to check. Because I have no practice taking independent excursions with my child.

Now what was I going to do? The Orbit is awesome, but it weighs—this is a rough estimate—a million pounds. Okay, it weighs almost ten pounds, but when you add that to my four-teen-pound baby, the total comes to almost a million pounds. (Math was never my strong subject.) I'd seen Dean carry it, but me? Never. Well, I had no choice, I was going to mom up and haul the thing through Neiman Marcus.

When I'm walking through Neiman Marcus I always feel like I'm being judged. As if the other shoppers are all so upscale that they're looking at me like I'm Julia Roberts in *Pretty Woman*— out of place and unwelcome. It seems to me that in a place like that you have to have a certain air of confidence that has never come easily to me. When I walked in with Stella, I didn't want anyone to look at me and think, "She can barely carry that child. She has no idea how to be a mother." So I was lugging her in her infant car seat up the escalator, dragging her from designer to designer, trying to act like it was effortless. In less than ten minutes my arm was aching, I was breaking a sweat, and my heart was pounding. Not cool, Tori, not cool. So I told myself I was doing an acting exercise. I concentrated on making my expression say to the other shoppers, "I'm a hands-on mom. This is no big deal. I'm just effortlessly shopping at Neiman Marcus. I do this all the time. I could run a marathon carrying this baby. And yours. Care to try me?"

I don't know what my face looked like, but at least my acting efforts distracted me from the pain. Soon enough I was happily ensconced in a dressing room, with Stella watching me try on dresses. As the salespeople brought me options, I explained the designers to Stella. "Look! A Christian Dior dress. Now, Stella, this is gorgeous but way out of our price range. But, here! Look at this—an Alice and Olivia. One dress is thousands of dollars, the other is three hundred dollars. Accessories are everything. If I pair the Alice and Olivia with this belt . . ." Stella loved it. The lights, the mirrors, the colors and patterns, and if I'm not mistaken she expressed great respect for the enduring style of the Diane von Furstenberg wrap dress.

Stella doesn't have a baby book. Before she was born I heard people talk about the second child syndrome—how number two doesn't get the same attention. I couldn't imagine that. Each baby was sure to be as precious as the last. But then, when Stella was born, I finally understood. The first four months of her life flew by, and suddenly I realized we had very little to show for it. No baby book, a few photos that were taken on my BlackBerry, and no record of her growth. By the time Liam was four months old I could have made twenty albums, one exclusively devoted to shots of him sleeping. I recorded every measurement the doctor took—height, weight, and head circumference. For Stella I only wrote down two measurements, her stats at birth and at her first doctor's visit.

Stella might grow up with no memories of her childhood, but I knew that we had a special bond from the very start. When day-old Stella stared up at me with her beautiful eyes, I couldn't help thinking, *This one's going to be mine!*

When you have a cesarean you stay in the hospital a few days. I slept a lot, held Stella, swaddled her, fed her. One afternoon Dean had gone to run some errands and Stella and I were alone. I was in the hospital bed holding her. She gazed right up at me. I know babies are basically blind for the first few days, but when she looked at me like that, I felt a deep connection to her. All of a sudden I had an epiphany. It was going to be okay. Everything was going to be fine. She was looking right into my soul to say, "I'm connecting with you, Mommy. We're going to love each other. We're going to have a great relationship. You're going to get me a car for my sixteenth birthday. I love you." I still feel that way when she looks at me. I feel the connection. Maybe I'm making it up because I want it so badly, but who cares? That feeling can't be a bad thing.

Now, in the dressing room at Neiman Marcus, I couldn't help fast-forwarding to years from now, to a day when I would watch Stella try on dresses, spinning around in front of the three-sided mirror. And that's when it hit me. Wow. I actually have a *girl*. And based on her response to the fashion show I'd just put on for her, she was going to be a shopper just like me.

Stella had remarkable shopping endurance. She was really good until the end. When she started to fuss, I knew it was time to book it out of there. I was still trying to decide between two dresses, so I bought them both with the plan to return the one I didn't wear.

Carrying Stella in her car seat into the store was hard enough. Now I was hustling to get out of there before she had a full-on meltdown, and I was carrying my purse, the diaper bag, the lead-weighted carrier, *and* the Neiman Marcus garment bag. As I trekked to the escalator, missing Sherpa Dean, a saleswoman looked at me, gasped, and said, "Oh my God, you must need

help! Let me take something." I instantly got super defensive. I
said, "No, why? [gasp, gasp] Do I look like I need help? [gasp,
gasp] I'm fine." I turned away, but she knew I was just being
stubborn. She said, "I'm a mom. It's okay to ask for help." I
knew that if Dean were alone with Stella, he'd never need an
extra hand. I wanted to prove the same independence. But my
arm muscles were already quivering under the weight, and I
was pretty sure this kind of exercise wasn't going to do much
for my postpartum love handles. So I reluctantly let her carry
the garment bag to the escalator. It was a moment of defeat. A
relieving, lifesaving, wonderful moment of defeat.

I fed Stella in the car, she perked up, and we hit Neil Lane.
Inside the brand-new store the counters were full of gleaming
jewelry. Stella's eyes opened wide. What was this place? She
had found her Shangri-la. As she gaped at the magnificent jewelry, I flashed back to my mother, who had such a fondness
for diamonds the size of race cars. As a teen I had begged her
to wear silver, crystal, plastic, cardboard—anything less showy.
She said, "One day you'll appreciate all these diamonds." Now
I was in a different situation, borrowing the jewelry that Mom
could buy, with a daughter whose four-month-old eyes lit up at
the sight of diamonds. I turned to Neil: "Do you have anything
in the macaroni necklace vein?" Still, I was proud. Stella and I
had our first independent excursion—borrowing jewelry from
the Hollywood diamond guy.

Of course, every happy story has a paparazzi ending. As we
drove away from the store they started tailing me, and all of a

sudden Stella started screaming in the back seat. I was reasonably sure this wasn't a late protest of my dress selection. She wanted another bottle. Like, now. I pulled over in a Petco parking lot, prepared the bottle, and stood there with the back door ajar, trying to feed the baby while hiding from the cameras. *Come on, Stella, we gotta go.* She seemed to finish up, but as soon as we got back on the road, she started screaming again. I was making up silly songs about the designers she'd seen, trying to find a way to rhyme "Dolce & Gabbana" with "Bottle's coming soon," but nothing was working. We had three paparazzi trailing us now, and if I stopped to take her out and comfort her, they would be all over us. I'm never hostile to the paparazzi. But I was so frazzled and irate with a screaming infant in the back seat that half a block from my house I lost it. I stopped the car, leaned out the window, and screamed, "Just fuck off!" to the guy behind me. The guy was shocked. He said, "Sorry, Tori." As soon as he said that, the road rage disappeared and I immediately felt guilty. That's right, guilty. About yelling at a paparazzo. Maybe I should have invited him back for a bottle of milk while I was at it.

Feeling cocky after my ninety percent successful outing with Stella, I was ready to try again. A couple of weeks later there was a sample sale for Splendid kids—an excellent but pricey line of kids' clothing. A group of celebrities was invited to go to a showroom in downtown Los Angeles to pick out ten outfits for the spring. It was a really good deal. The sale fell on Patsy's birthday and we had a big dinner planned with her gays (my gays were her gays now). So after I finished up my meetings for the day, the two kids and I set off for downtown L.A. to do a little shopping before we met up with Patsy's dinner party. That's right—me and my two kids. Every mother should be able to handle her own two children, right? It would be double bonus bonding time.

It took us an hour to get downtown. Both kids were fussing. It was a nightmare. By the time we got downtown it was dark. We parked in a scary underground garage. (Did I mention that I'm scared of downtown? I am. It can be a dangerous place, but I'm probably scared about four hours earlier than everyone else gets scared.) By the time we got upstairs to the sale, I only had fifteen minutes before our dinner reservations. It wasn't exactly a leisurely shopping situation.

The showroom was pretty small. I was rushing around with Stella in the double stroller. Liam was running in circles. At some point I looked up from the clothes to check on Liam. I found him surrounded by a group of tall, beautiful, model-type girls. They were feeding him M&M's. They apologized, but I said it was okay for him to have a few. Then, as I watched, Liam started feeding the women M&M's. They were bending down and Liam, who never, ever shares food, was putting M&M's into the mouths of the models—who probably never, ever ate M&M's—and loving it. The kid has good instincts.

Finally we left—so late for dinner already!—and I realized that I had no cash to pay for the garage. The security guard told me there was an ATM out on the corner. It was dark. I was scared. But I stood at the ATM, holding Stella, trying to make a withdrawal. Meanwhile Liam wanted to explore. He strayed away from the ATM, first just a step or two, then a bit further. I could see bums halfway down the block. Liam wasn't wandering far, but what was safe? It would only take a second for someone to scoop him up and run away. I kept telling Liam to come back to me. He just thought it was a very funny game.

Finally, cash in hand, I loaded the kids into the car. All I needed to do was fold up the double stroller, put it in the back, and hurry to dinner. Now this double stroller—Dean always deals with it. He's the stroller unfolder. But now it was up to me and I couldn't do it. The two little things—you're supposed to unclick them—I knew exactly what to do, but the stupid thing would not unclick. Liam was flushed and hungry. And Stella was screaming bloody murder because if there's anything Stella hates it's a car that isn't moving. I tried calling Dean several times for tips, moral support, anything! But he was on the set of a TV movie. I tried to jam the stroller into the back without folding it, at full mast, but the back door wouldn't close. Literally twenty minutes later (dinner! Patsy! our gays!) I was dripping in sweat. It was hopeless.

I'd had it. I looked and my watch and said to the empty (scary! dark!) garage, "We have to go. We have to leave the stroller." I felt bad. The stroller was so expensive. I knew Dean would have managed to fold it. But resigned, I wheeled the stroller to an out-of-the-way corner of the garage and left it there. Someone would take it. Someone who needed it more. Someone who didn't get it for free just for being a celebrity.

I made one halfhearted effort to find the stroller a good home: when we pulled up to the exit, I asked the cashier if he knew someone who needed a stroller. He spoke not a word of English. We were so late. We just left.

Downtown is a mess of one-way streets, all going the wrong direction. I had no idea how to get on the freeway. So I just drove, hoping to see a sign. Then I heard Liam cough. I looked back. "Are you okay?" He coughed again. Then he turned bright red. Was he choking? Was he having a seizure? Was he ODing from M&M's? (Can you OD from M&M's?) I was about to pull over (which should give you some idea of how panicked I was, since pulling over in downtown L.A. at night meant certain death as far as I was concerned), when all of a sudden Liam got distracted by a billboard with some animals on it and stopped. He was totally faking.

Then it was Stella's turn. She started screaming and didn't stop. It was excruciating. I knew from experience that with Stella and the car there were only two options: she'd scream the whole way, or she'd scream until she fell asleep. Stella screamed the entire way in bumper-to-bumper traffic. So much for the free Splendid outfits. They were adorable, but I doubt our ordeal was really worth it. It cost me a stroller, and even worse, ever since Liam met those M&M-feeding models, he demands candy—to the point of a tantrum—whenever he enters a clothing store.

That night, after Patsy's party, when Dean and I were getting ready for bed, I broke it to him about the stroller. So my second shopping expedition wasn't as successful as the first. But remember when I was too self-conscious to throw away the poop-covered swim towel at Liam's swimming lesson? Well, I was making great progress in deserting expensive personal possessions. Okay, so that wasn't my goal, but the point is that I was feeling more confident about my decisions. I was in charge, and even if my choices weren't always frugal, at least I was starting to take the lead.

Our relationships with our children are always works in progress. I'll never forget or let go of my concerns about being a mother, especially to a girl. In the back of my mind I'll always be asking, *How am I doing with Stella? Am I handling this right? Am I being competitive or judgmental?* Our time together and how we spend it—even when she's an infant—add up to the relationship we'll have when she's a grown woman. Not that she'll remember her first year or two or, for that matter, which designers I showcased on any particular excursion, but whatever her first memories end up being, I want them to be fond and happy. I want her to think, *I know my mom always loved me. She had to work, but I remember always having a great relationship with her.*

As for Liam, my little Daddy's boy, this morning Dean and I both woke up when he started crying. I waited a beat, expecting Dean to fly out of bed as always. Instead, Dean said, "Oh, he's up." I said, "Yeah, yeah, he just woke up." Dr. Wexler had told us that Dean had to sit back and give me the opportunity to do more, and here he was, giving me a chance to be the one who brought Liam that morning's bottle. I took it. I loved going through that door and seeing Liam's first smile of the morning, accepting his first hug. A few minutes later, as I changed his poo-filled diaper, I thought, "And why exactly did I want to do this?"

Almost Normal

One evening Liam and I were walking down the street having some mother-son alone time. Now, Liam shows absolutely no signs of having inherited my shyness. So when he saw a kid from across the street go into our neighbor's backyard, he trotted right along behind him. I saw that a small group of neighbors was gathered while the kids scampered around the yard. I asked if it was okay if we came in, and they were completely nice and welcoming.

So I stood there with the other moms and dads, chatting the way neighbors do about this and that. An everyday moment in a mainstream neighborhood. I could see that they were trying to be nice to me. No, that's not it exactly. They were trying to be *normal* to me. But you could feel it in the air: I was different, but they didn't want me to think they thought I was different, so they were treating me . . . differently. And I was part of the same act. I was trying to act normal, trying to act like a mom. Of course I *was* a mom, but I wanted them to see that I was a *normal* mom. It didn't matter that I'd lost most of the baby weight. There was an elephant in the room (in the backyard, anyway), and it was me.

One of the moms said, "Oh, we're applying for this preschool. We went to look at it last week." She looked at me to include me, and I said that we were thinking about preschools too. She said, "Oh yes, we know you're looking for preschools; we saw it on the show last week." Then there was an awkward silence. She was embarrassed that she'd brought up the fact that they all already knew what was going on in my life. I was embarrassed that she was embarrassed. It shouldn't be a big deal. I have a reality show. I know that people—even my neighbors, maybe especially my neighbors—watch it. Then when we meet in real life, everyone wants the encounter to feel normal and it just doesn't. It isn't anyone's fault.

Remember the woman who welcomed us to the neighborhood with flowers from her garden and homemade brownies? Well, we'd never really talked since. Sometimes I saw the other moms gathered on her lawn. They stood in a group and talked while their kids ran around. A couple of times I milled around in our driveway hoping for someone to invite me over, but it never happened. Occasionally I'd run into another neighbor who'd say, "Next time I'm going to ring your doorbell at five and drag you over there," but she never did. I didn't feel comfortable, didn't want to come over uninvited or to intrude. But what if they'd been saying, "She never came. What's she doing, waiting for an engraved invitation?"

Does being known have to be awkward? Maybe I'm the one who makes it so. When you add my insecurities about being a good mother to the expectation that I'm not a normal mother, you get awkwardness and embarrassment all around. I think about that time when Liam pooped in the pool during swim class. I walked over to the side of the pool to get my diaper bag. There were two other moms sitting around. The coach said to me, loudly, from across the pool, "I hope whoever packed your diaper bag today put a lot of wipes in there!" But I had packed my own diaper bag. It would never even occur to me to ask someone to pack my diaper bag. I wanted to shout back, "Um, nobody packs my diaper bag for me, Coach!" but I knew that would just sound odd and defensive. The coach wasn't being rude. She's the nicest woman in the world. She just assumed that since I'm a celebrity who has help, there was probably someone who that morning cooked my breakfast, did my dishes, and wiped my ass for me. As I left the house, someone with a checklist and an earpiece probably hung my diaper bag over my shoulder, saying, "Diapers: check. Wipes: check. Butt paste: check." And as soon as I walked back in the door, someone would take the bag off my shoulder, clean and refill it.

I'm exaggerating. I hope. I'm sure the swim coach doesn't think my life is so fancy. But she assumes I'm living a "celebrity life." She doesn't really feel like we have anything in common. But what moms should I connect with? I mean, I don't really relate to other celebrities. Or I relate to other celebrities the same way noncelebrities relate to me. I'm like, *Ooh, there's a celebrity. Try to act normal!* When I cohosted *The View,* Kate Winslet was the guest that day. Backstage, before we went on, she started chatting with me. As we were talking I kept saying to myself, "Just act normal. She's the star of *Titanic!* Just act normal." We started talking about breastfeeding, and the whole time all I could think was "I'm talking to Kate Winslet, the star of *Titanic,* about breastfeeding." I couldn't separate the person in front of me from the person on the big screen. Is that how people feel with me? That confusion between the pleasant stranger in front of them and everything else they know about me? Meanwhile, Kate Winslet seemed perfectly comfortable with me. She knew stuff about my life too. She knew Liam's name. She didn't seem the least bit self-conscious. But who knows what was going through her mind. If I were her, I know it would have been, "Oh my God, *I'm* Kate Winslet! The star of *Titanic!* And I'm talking about breastfeeding!"

I don't relate any differently than most people to celebrities, but there does seem to be some sort of expectation that we have a connection just because we're all in the public eye. Recently I got an email that my publicist had forwarded from Sean Combs's head assistant. It said that my family was invited to a birthday party for Puff's twins, Jessie and D'Lila. Sean and Kim were having a birthday party for their children and wanted to invite Ms. Tori Spelling and family.

Now, I'd never met Diddy. As far as I knew, I'd never even

been in the same room as him. I emailed all my friends, "How Hollywood is this?" I had a fantasy of him asking his assistant for a list of every celebrity parent in Los Angeles, then going down the list saying, "Approved. Not Approved. Approved. Not Approved." I really had no idea why the invitation had come. It was just so random. But if I was invited, that had to mean that hundreds of other people were invited. It was going to be gigantic. I had to go.

As it happened, we had plans for the day of the party with Scout and Bill. Could they come? The invitation said "Tori Spelling and family." Scout and Bill were family. We call them the Guncles. I asked my publicist to find out if we could bring them. She wrote back, "No problem. You're all on the list." Scout said that he was coming for the gift bag alone.

The party was being held from one to five at an estate in Beverly Hills. That morning Dean and I went out to pick up a present for the twins. (I had to look online to figure out that they were both girls. How's that for a sign that you don't really belong at a birthday party—not knowing the gender of the guests of honor?) Presents for one-year-old twins—how hard could that be? But as we went from store to store we were stymied. These were girls who probably had everything. Every toy. Every outfit. I decided that clothes were the way to go. Girls can't have too many clothes. But how did Diddy dress his daughters? Did twins have to match? I had almost settled on an outfit when Dean said they were going to expect a certain level of style from me. My gift had to stand out. It was back to the drawing table. Finally, after going to five stores, we picked out two outfits. One was all pinks. The other matched but was in purples. There were little socks, barrettes, and rubber duckie kits. I nervously wrote out each card: "Dear D'Lila, Happy first birthday. We wish you all the best. Love, Tori Spelling, Dean McDermott, Liam, and Stella." I had to put our last names, otherwise they might not know whose gift it was. Same thing for Jessie. By the time everything was wrapped and ready we'd spent half our day on the birthday presents.

Stella was napping, so we left her at home with Patsy. I dressed Liam in jeans, an argyle sweater, and a black velvet blazer. He had product in his hair. It was his first big-time celebrity birthday party (excluding his own, of course).

The party was at a huge mansion belonging to Ron Burkle, the billionaire business magnate. Paparazzi were gathered at the gate. We dropped off our car with the valet, climbed two driveways, then walked through two tunnels out to the backyard. It was a good fifteen-minute walk in heels. Who wears heels to a children's party? Big mistake. So I was struggling, but Liam was fine. He was looking around the grounds, wide-eyed. Maybe he was having flashbacks to his few, fading memories of his visits to my mother's house.

When we got to the backyard, the first thing we saw was a station where we were meant to get Polaroid pictures taken of ourselves as a souvenir of the party. But we were late—all those hours present-shopping—and nobody was manning the table. While we stood there, a little lost, I noticed that the sign at

the table said, "Get your souvenir picture taken at the twins'
second birthday party." Second? I had assumed it was their first
birthday! And the email invitation hadn't specified how old
the twins were. My carefully penned birthday card was wrong.
The clothes were the wrong size. I didn't know what to do. I
was mortified. So I took out a pen (wrong color!), crossed out
"first" and wrote "second" on both cards. Just then an assistant
came up and welcomed us. I shoved our presents to the middle
of the pile and tried to put them out of my mind. We smiled
for a picture in front of a fountain with the sprawling lawn
behind us.

We followed the assistant down what felt like a hedge lab-
yrinth until we heard voices. We turned a corner and found
ourselves on a lawn where little kids sat in a circle watching an
odd man do a puppet show. Diddy sat on a chair with a girl on
each knee. The puppet master made some reference to Gomer
Pyle, and a Rogaine joke. Huh? Well, his material may have
been a little age-inappropriate, but the two-year-olds seemed to
be enjoying themselves, especially Liam, who had pulled Dean
right into the circle.

Bill scurried off for drinks and came back with plastic princess cups with spiked princess punch (adults only, of course!).
I must have made a face when I tasted the punch, because Bill
asked if I'd rather have wine. I said sure, and moments later he
returned with my wine. But it wasn't in a plastic princess cup
like everyone else's drinks. The wine was in a large, crystal gob-
let. As I took my first sip I looked around and saw that I was

the only mom drinking wine. Conspicuously. I took a couple of sips, then hid the wine in the bushes, whispering, "I'll come back for you later."

Bill, Scout, and I stood back to assess the attendees. The only people we recognized were two soap stars and Gwen Stefani and her family. There were about fifty guests in total. Wait a minute—fifty guests? Sure, that's a big party for two-year-olds, but it was nothing compared to what I'd expected. How in the world did I make it onto the list?

Just then Diddy came up to us. He greeted us, thanked us for coming, and shook everyone's hand, making sure to meet and welcome each of us. He was warm and pleasant. I had assumed that a mogul like him would be too busy for us, but at his daughters' birthday party he seemed like a parent just like any of us, taking time to greet all the guests. I guess I get why people have preconceived notions of me; I seem to have them of other people too. Diddy couldn't have been nicer and more genuine.

When the puppet show was over it was cake time. Liam loves singing "Happy Birthday." Dean held him up to see the cake. Liam leaned forward, trying to blow out the candles. It was really cute, and it all felt perfectly nice and normal, except I still couldn't figure out what I was doing there.

Then Kim, the birthday girls' mother, came over to me with another woman; I gathered it was her friend and assistant. They introduced themselves and then Kim told me that *Tori & Dean* was her favorite show. She said, "I've watched every episode. I love your family. And I loved it when you decorated that house. You have the best style." Aha! Now I got it. I was there because Kim felt like she knew me (or would like to know me) through our show. When they were making the party list she must have thought, "Well, I like Tori and Dean, and I like Gwen Stefani. I'll invite them." It had never occurred to me that I could invite anyone I was interested in to Liam's birthday parties. I could invite Gwen Stefani. Heck, I could even invite Kate Winslet!

Kim said, "We should have a playdate with the kids," and we exchanged emails. Then her assistant said, "Or the nannies. The nannies can get the kids together."

The party was winding down. We circled past the petting zoo, the carousel, and the miniature horse rides. There was a nice buffet, a cappuccino/hot chocolate bar, a cotton candy machine, and popcorn. Not as over-the-top as I thought it would be. But yeah, my standards are a little warped.

I'd been texting Mehran about Gwen Stefani's presence since he worships her. He wanted me to go up to her. "You have the same agent!" he was texting. "Just say hi!" I've never walked up to a total stranger and introduced myself, but for Mehran I sucked it up. She had baby Zuma in a sling. I asked how old he was, and how her older son, Kingston, was reacting to the baby. I wondered if it was weird that I knew her children's names. But then she said, "How's your daughter?" and I realized she knew I had a daughter. It's just part of our world that people, including other celebrities, know our kids' names. We talked about babies and siblings for a few minutes, and then we had nothing else to talk about and said good-bye.

As we left we picked up our souvenir picture, which was now mounted on pink paper and said, in purple, "Thank you for coming to D'Lila and Jessie's party." We also scooped up the gift bag that had Scout so excited. Other guests started rifling through their gift bags in the tunnel on the way to the valet, but we restrained ourselves until we got into the car. The bag contained a pink crown cookie on a stick, a plush doll, an educational children's DVD, a baby sling, and a child-sized T-shirt with the twins' names and faces on it. Poor Scout. It wasn't exactly what he had in mind.

I suppose if Gwen Stefani and I had had more time or we'd been in different circumstances, we might have found commonalities, but the chances weren't smaller or greater that I would hit it off with her than with any other mom. There's no instant celebrity bond. The truth is that ninety percent of my life is the same as everyone else's: I go to work every day. I love my husband, we have disagreements, we continue to love each other and try to make our time together special. I have friends who mean the world to me and who annoy me and who help me navigate my life. And I'm especially like everyone else when it comes to the mommying parts. I worry about my kids when they're sleeping; I try to get them to eat the right foods; I hope they're having fun as they start to make sense of the world; I want them to make friends, to grow, to thrive, to love and be loved. I really want to connect and talk and commiserate with others about it all, and it's kind of a bummer that celebrity—that other ten percent of my life—always seems to get in the way.

When we moved to Beaver Avenue, my fantasy was to be in a kid-friendly neighborhood where Dean and I would become friends with the parents of Liam's—and eventually Stella's— friends. I wanted a community. I wanted the whole suburban dream that was so foreign to me growing up in a huge house with a long driveway that no trick-or-treaters would bother to hike. Our house on Beaver Avenue was everything I thought I wanted.

But our house was right on the street. There was no fence, no hedge, and no privacy. Our show means cameras are in our kitchen, our bedroom, our backyard. I'm constantly exposed (without makeup), but for some reason the show doesn't feel like an invasion of privacy. I guess the notion that it is transmitted by cables and satellites creates kind of a buffer between us and the people who are watching us. They might see us, but I can't see them.

Meanwhile, when I walked out the front door of our house, I saw curtains open as people peeped out at me. One day when I was walking Stella, a woman came up to us and said, "Hi, Stella Doreen!" Then she said, "I'm sorry to bother you. I can see you're out walking your baby. But I just wanted to say that I love the show." I thanked her and was about to walk on when she said, "Can I ask what you're doing in this neighborhood?" A little taken aback, I said, "I live a block away." She said, "I'd never have thought you'd live in our neighborhood!" She was right. I didn't belong. Not because I was too rich or too famous or too snobby. But because none of us could get past the fact of who I was. Nobody was comfortable, including me.

Not long after we moved in, Jack was back in L.A. and spending much more time with us. Though we had planned for Jack to sleep in the den, we started regretting that we didn't have another bedroom in the house that he could call his own. We wanted to make sure he felt at home. Then there's the fact that Dean and I work out of our house. There are always extra people—producers and cameramen—moving around us as we go about our lives. Our house was plenty big for a family of four, but it didn't fit the life we were living now.

You always want what you don't have. Growing up, I always wanted a small house. I wanted a cozy space where I could feel close to my family. Honestly, just a place where I could find my parents without using an intercom would have been an improvement. But now we wanted a room for Jack and an office for me and Dean and more space for those cameras to glide by without bumping into corners or small children. If we moved just outside L.A., over the hill where real estate was less expensive, we could trade our house for one that was big enough for our family and job, and gated to keep the paparazzi at bay.

All I ever wanted was to be normal, to raise my kids as a normal mom in a normal house in a normal neighborhood. But my dreams of normal were crashing into the reality of our family's special situation. Having paparazzi assault us every time we left the house wasn't normal. Having neighbors peek out windows at us when we came out the front door wasn't normal. Being followed as we drove away wasn't normal. I was beginning to realize that the normal I'd been seeking wasn't a matter of living in the right neighborhood or bringing the right cake to the block party or walking across the street to hang out with the neighbors uninvited. "Normal" was a concept that was mostly in my head, and the best way to achieve it was to build a life where we were calm and comfortable and felt at peace. There were other factors, of course, but I knew for certain that that life wasn't happening on Beaver Avenue.

If we lived in a normal house, we would have no privacy. If we lived in a private house, we would lose the friendly neighborhood. We had to find a compromise. The new house we found was the compromise. Dean and I basically traded location for space. The new house would make Jack more comfortable, which was high on our list of reasons to move. It was closer to him and Mary Jo. It was set back from the road, with a security gate that kept paparazzi at a distance. We'd be able to get into our cars without being photographed. The rooms were on a bigger scale, which meant we wouldn't be tripping over light cords and cameramen as we lived our lives in front of the lens. There was a big, grassy backyard where our children could crawl and toddle now, and later run and play tag and have a swing set. And there were neighbors, but not so close that they could see in our windows. We may have wanted a close-knit, friendly relationship with our neighbors, but we needed privacy and safety. Maybe here we would find the balance.

When I showed the house to Jenny and Mehran, they were excited. Mehran called it my first grown-up house. Jenny was like, "This is going to be so great. Our kids will all play in this backyard together. During the summer our kids will be splashing around in the pool. We'll celebrate holidays here together." She saw it as I did, a place where my family and friendships would grow, a place where we would all create memories together. That was exactly the reaction I was hoping for, but it wasn't the only reaction I heard.

My makeup artist has worked with me for years and years. When I showed her the website for the new house (this is common in L.A.), her reaction was, "Now *this* is the type of house I'd expect Tori Spelling to live in." Hearing that crushed me. To me it meant that the house was a rich-girl mansion, the right house for the daughter of megamogul Aaron Spelling. I felt embarrassed, ashamed. I'd worked my whole life to get to a certain place, a place where people saw me as a normal person. I know my makeup artist cares about me, and she didn't mean it in a bad way, but what she said tapped into my greatest fears. After all that work, proving that I was an independent, self-supporting, hardworking actor, when I moved into this house I'd be forever pigeonholed as the overentitled, spoiled rich girl everyone has always assumed I was. I worked hard to earn the money to buy that house, and part of me was proud of what I'd achieved, but the rest of me was just devastated that I could never escape the preconceived notion of how Tori Spelling would live.

Red Carpet Drama

Everyone's got a central conflict in their lives, a constant theme that their personal struggles and problems keep coming back to visit. In case you haven't figured out mine yet, this is it: part of me wants to escape the life that Tori Spelling is expected to live, and part of me is so used to that life that I can't imagine anything else. Red carpet events have always been a standard component of my social life. I'm so accustomed to entering an event that way, for me it's almost as mindless as putting the car into park. I just do it without thinking.

There are certain expectations on the red carpet. Your hair will be done. Your makeup will be perfect. You'll have a fresh manicure and pedicure. You will be wearing designer clothes and will be able to correctly pronounce the name of each designer. You'll know how to stand in a flattering pose. Your date, whose outfit requires nearly equal attention but will receive no reaction whatsoever, will pose with you, then step out of the frame for the "fashion shot." You'll answer questions in quick, friendly sound bites, with smiles and a bit of humor, wait for the final flashes, then head into the event without delay. It's old hat to me.

And then came Liam. But before I talk about Liam's first red carpet experience, I want to take a moment to discuss Liam's socialization, such as it is. I want to talk about boobies.

There came the day (and believe me, I thought it would be much later in his development) when Liam started wondering what my boobs were. He'd come up to me and push on them inquisitively. Dean would say, "Mama's boobies." I figured now was a good time for him to understand the human body, long before he got all caught up in adolescent drama. So I'd lift my shirt and say, "Mama has boobies. Daddy and Liam have nipples." Same as you'd show your kid your belly button: "Mama has an innie on a perfectly flat tummy." (I wish!) "Daddy has an outie." (Dean: exposed!) He got it down pretty quickly, so when I said, "Where are Mama's boobies?" he'd say, "Boobies!" lift my shirt, and come in for the honk.

Liam's booby grab was my favorite baby show-off trick. Scout and Bill loved it. As for Mehran, well, Mehran had issues. He regretted my boob job. He's always said that I'd wear designer clothes much better if I didn't have the boobs. He'll say, "One size smaller—would you ever consider it? It'd be so much easier to dress you." Mehran has a point. In the nineties, when I bought the boobs, they looked great with the clothes, but they don't wear today's fashion well. (I can only hope they come back into style someday.) But that wasn't my real regret about the procedure. I've said before and I'll say again that if I'd known when I was twenty-one that implants could impair my ability to produce enough milk for my babies, I wouldn't have gotten them. That leaves Dean as the only supporter with no regrets. Dean loves them. And Liam is his Daddy's little boy. When Liam reached for the goods, Dean would say, "That's my boy! You like Mommy's boobies just like Daddy."

It was all very cute and innocent—until the Public Booby Incident. I brought Liam to the playground one day and was sitting around the other moms and nannies while the kids played. Then Liam started saying, "Boobies! Boobies!" and trying to lift my shirt. I turned red and struggled to keep my shirt down, "Liam, not now!" Poor kid, he was just trying to play the game that Dean and I love and encourage at home, and now Mama was withholding. Liam started getting really frustrated, trying to lift my shirt and chanting, "Boobies, boobies!" more and more emphatically. He was on the verge of a full-blown tantrum. I stood up (so as to be out of reach) and redirected his attention to the slide. But as I looked around, it seemed that everyone at the playground was trying really hard to *not* look at me, and they were all a little farther away from me than they'd been before the Incident. I guess some things that are funny at home aren't acceptable out in the real world. Is it too early for him to learn that lesson? Because I have to admit, I still think it's funny.

It's becoming all too clear to me that Liam, and eventually Stella, are kids who are going to have ample opportunities to embarrass their parents. Or rather, we're setting them up to embarrass us. For instance, we were on our way to an event to protest Proposition 8 (the ban on gay marriage in California). When we stepped out of the house—we were still on Beaver Avenue—we saw our neighbors with their son, Sam. Sam is really cute with Liam. He always wants Liam to come over to play tag or catch. So when Sam yelled, "Can Liam come over and play?" we decided we weren't in a hurry and there was time for the boys to run around together.

Now, Liam was all duded up for the event in True Religion jeans, a Lucky Brand shirt, and gold L.A.M.B. shoes (from Gwen Stefani's children's line). Sam was out there with his mom and another adult. The two boys were kicking the ball around. Then Sam's mom said, "Look at those gold shoes!" I was embarrassed. I have different styles for different situations. It's like I do costume changes. I have my "mom" outfits, with flip-flops and jeans, and my "going to be photographed" outfits, and my "fashion event" outfits. This may sound nuts, but Liam kind of has the same setup: he has different wardrobes for different contexts. I knew that at a Hollywood event, people—especially the "No on 8" gays—would see his gold shoes and say, "Aw, he looks fierce." But in a normal suburban neighborhood they were probably a bit much. I nervously laughed and racked my mind for a situation-appropriate joke. I didn't want to mention the Prop 8 rally. Who knew what her politics were? I didn't want to sound defensive. She wasn't being mean, she was just noticing the shoes. I was the one who was insecure and trying to make sure she didn't think I wanted Liam to be a tricked-out toddler (most of the time). Finally I just said, "When in your life can you wear gold shoes without being mocked if not under the age of two?" She chuckled kindly. Phew.

But for the record, Liam looked awesome in his gold shoes. Thank you, Gwen Stefani.

The Prop 8 protest wasn't a unique occasion; we were starting to bring Stella and Liam along to just about all the events we attended. Or more accurately, we stopped going to most events, and the only ones we managed to get to were kid-friendly. I haven't been to a movie premiere in ages. I'd rather stay at home on premiere night and go later, with my husband, in sweatpants, without makeup and four-inch heels. One week it was the Prop 8 protest. The following week we had two events: Jenny McCarthy's autism benefit at the Treehouse Social Club, a cute playspace café in Beverly Hills, and a charity event at Build-A-Bear, benefiting the Ronald McDonald House.

Dressing for an event was always a fashion project, but bringing both babies for the first time complicated matters even more. I had to think through how the red carpet would go. When I knew I was going to be carrying the kids, my instinct was to be in my mom wardrobe. I always wear flats, flip-flops, or sneakers as a mom. But I knew that at an event, photos would be taken. The magazines would scrutinize my outfit and assess my postbaby weight loss. Heels elongate legs, make you look thinner, and are more fashionably accepted. I had to wear heels. Still, I couldn't exactly walk around for two hours wearing Christian Louboutin stilettos, holding a baby and chasing a toddler. That was ridiculous. So what was the happy medium? Wedges. I'd wear wedges. But I couldn't help wondering how the other celebrity moms did it. I always saw photos of Katie Holmes in four-inch heels with Suri. What was her secret? Did she dump those gorgeous shoes in the gutter the minute the photos were taken? I had to wonder. I'll ask Kate Winslet next time we chat.

I wore jeans to both events that week, with a cardigan and wedges one day and a soft black cashmere sweater and boots the next. After they took the family shot, Dean would step out of picture for the female-only fashion shot. But I was going to be so casual that I worried the outfits weren't fashion-worthy enough for the magazines. When I go to an event, I feel like I have to wear an outfit that garners some degree of fashion praise. In all my ventures, especially the clothing and jewelry companies, being Tori Spelling—fashionable Tori Spelling—is my business. What if they said I'd lost my passion for fashion? What if I wasn't even a "Fashion Don't"? What if I was just a "Didn't Bother"? Well, I was wearing what I was wearing, so I'd find out the hard way.

In the days leading up to the Build-A-Bear event, Liam was starting to discover his little sister. It was really sweet . . . except when it wasn't. On Friday night Dean and Liam were sitting on the couch in the family room watching cartoons. I came in and sat down with Stella. I said, "Look, Monkey. Buggy's here. She's going to watch cartoons with you." As I watched I saw Liam, his eyes still focused on the TV screen, reach over and slowly take Stella's hand. I couldn't believe it. I caught Dean's eye and mouthed to him, "Look!" It was the cutest thing I'd ever seen, my two small children holding hands. (And, yes, watching TV together, but we're a TV family, what can I do?) Dean and I were blissing out on our moment of family love.

Then, as I watched, the hand holding got increasingly enthusiastic. Liam squeezed Stella's hand tighter and tighter until she started screaming. I extracted her and hid my panic while I assessed the damage. Was her hand broken? Would she ever recover? Was hand modeling a career she'd have to forsake? Then Liam started in; he doesn't like when Stella cries. Family love was transformed in an instant to family grief. Eventually everyone calmed down and, total collapse aside, we decided that holding hands was a giant step. Liam had noticed Stella. He was injuring her. They were turning into real siblings.

The next day I put Stella on the bed with Liam. Usually when I put her next to him, he pushes her away, but this time he started petting her head. I said, "Is this your baby?" and he nodded. Then he started to get excited and said, "Baby, baby!" and pointed at her. Then he started playing a game where he'd go up close to her face and say "Boo!" She thought it was hysterical, which got Liam more excited, and the more excited he was, the rougher he was. Finally, since at this age all things fun must end in tears, he did it one too many times, hit her in face, and she started crying. Game over.

The point is, the whole weekend we saw the two kids connecting. He rolled on top of her and made her cry. He bit her foot and made her cry. He grabbed her and made her cry. We clearly had to work on the whole gentle thing, but he was really interacting with her. And Stella at five months looked at Liam with such adoration. You could just see the years ahead, that she was going to look up to him as a big brother and a hero for the rest of her life.

After that auspicious weekend, we brought both babies to the Build-A-Bear event at Hollywood and Highland, where the Oscars take place. It was Stella's first red carpet appearance. I had her in my arms. Liam was really excited. He loves walking the red carpet. But then he saw a kiosk with an Elmo puppet. He fixated on the Elmo. We wanted to keep things moving smoothly, so we bought it for him. But then Liam decided that he absolutely didn't want to go into Build-A-Bear. That took us by surprise. We pointed at the bears in the window. Could any child resist so many cute, furry bears? One child could: Liam. And when I say didn't want to go, well, we're talking full-fledged terrible twos meltdown. Dean was holding Liam, but Liam was arching and screaming, trying to get down. You know, classic grocery store tantrum. Except we weren't in the grocery store. We were surrounded by celebrities in fancy dress and cameramen ready to document this particular tantrum to be filed and resuscitated ad nauseam for the rest of Liam's life. Maybe suitable for his private, extended family video montage, but not for the general public.

Dean put the squirming child down, and Liam hurled himself face-first onto the red carpet, screaming and crying. I said, "Don't worry, Liam, Tara Reid did the same thing on the red carpet last week." A paparazzo looked at me and said, "Really?" Oh, come on, seriously people. It was a *joke*. I said, "No, I'm just trying to make light of the fact that my son is having a tantrum on the red carpet, you're taking pictures, and I'm completely embarrassed."

At home when Liam has tantrums I talk him through them. I kneel down next to him and calmly say the stuff that moms say: "I know you're frustrated and can't find words. It's okay to be upset. Try to use your words. When you can pull yourself together we can go and have fun." I articulate his situation because I know he can't explain his feelings. But this time we weren't at home. We were surrounded by people documenting the situation. The unspoken understanding between me and Dean was that we didn't want to make this a big deal. The more we called attention to the tantrum, the more of a big deal they would make it in the press. (Thanks in advance, *TMZ*.) Liam wouldn't care now, but one day he might. We'd just let the tantrum run its course. We hoped that would happen quickly and when he recovered, we'd move on. And that's what happened.

Someone rushed up to us and handed Liam a Build-A-Bear. (Great, my son was now being rewarded for his wonderful behavior.) Liam paused to examine his new friend, and just like that, the tantrum was over. Calm was restored to the red carpet. I looked at Liam. He was puffy-eyed and red-cheeked, and his hair was mussed. In my head I made some Nick Nolte mug shot joke. Poor Liam was still trying to catch his breath. I thought maybe tapping into his new love affair with Stella would pull him the rest of the way out of his funk. I said, "Look, Liam, Buggy wants to see your new Build-A-Bear." He turned toward us and the twenty paparazzi and smashed Stella on the head with the bear. He wasn't joking. He was mad. Turns out I had tapped into his love-*hate* affair with Stella. Luckily, Stella just giggled. Good times, good times. And after that cathartic bear bonk, Liam was fully recovered.

If Liam pulled this kind of stunt at a movie premiere, I'd question our judgment in taking a child to an adult event, but this was a charity event at Build-A-Bear. We went because we thought it would be a fun family outing for a great cause. The red carpet tantrum—it had to happen. It's practically required for admission to Mommywood. I had been initiated.

Dean and I talked about it later. What was the right parenting approach to that moment? Some parents might say you should parent the way you parent regardless of the cameras. We're hip to that; we do it all the time in front of the reality show cameras. But in this case we decided that minimizing the moment was more important. Protecting Liam from the exposure took precedence over walking him through the tantrum. Every parent has to choose her battles. Ours were not going to be fought in public. I decided that the red carpet tantrum is a close cousin to the airplane tantrum. You just try to get through it with minimal trauma to all concerned. And (if you ignore the bear bribe and the abuse of Stella) he kind of worked through it himself and recovered quite quickly. Though maybe I should consider full-body armor for Stella. If they make it in pink.

So Long, Jägermeister Shots

Most of our life isn't on the red carpet, of course. Remember? Ninety percent normal. Like most couples who become parents, Dean and I talk about how having kids has changed us. I love the way our days begin. Our morning ritual is that when Liam wakes up, we bring him into our bed. We put him between the two of us, give him his morning bottle. (Yes, he still gets one bottle in the morning. Don't judge me!) We all watch cartoons together. As soon as Liam finishes his bottle, he leaps off the bed to sit in his little chair and watch TV from there. Sometimes when Liam's sitting there, happily in TVland, Dean gets a little . . . frisky. I whisper, "Liam's here. Liam's watching," and generally manage to put him off. But one morning I succumbed and we started to have sex. What can I say? There's just something about SpongeBob. We were under the covers being really quiet. But at some point I turned over and saw that Liam was standing at the side of the bed watching us.

Oh my God. Had we scarred him forever? They say TV is bad for kids! One minute he was sitting in his chair innocently watching SpongeBob and the next he was staring at us, and we were not rated G. Actually, a talking cleaning product is pretty creepy. It's hard to say which scene was more disturbing. We stopped (of course!). Dean said, "Oh, he's fine. Good for him!" But I promptly got on the web and started Googling "primal scene" to find out what kind of damage seeing his parents having sex would do to a then one-year-old. The news wasn't good. All I could figure out was that some child Freud treated had an image in his head of his parents having sex and became a neurotic known as the Wolf Man. Good-bye, Monkey, hello, Wolf Man. Or maybe Liam thought Dean was hurting me and would rise to protect and defend me. I *was* sort of hoping Liam would have a mild case of oedipal complex and would shift his affections from Dean to me. But this wasn't exactly how I had planned for it to come about.

This incident aside, I didn't think having children was cramping our sex life the way everyone said it would. Dean and I were sitting around a table with some of the producers from our show. We were talking about sex after babies, and one of the other married men at the table said, "*What* sex life after kids?" Dean and I have sex three to four times a week! Impressive, right? But Dean isn't so convinced. He always says, "Remember when we met? We had sex three times a day every single day."

Okay, but come on! Who can maintain that? Dean says, "When we first met, you couldn't keep your hands off me. If I came on to you at three in the morning, you were into it, but now you're always tired. You seem more in love with your bed." Well, duh! Before we had kids we could sleep in till one in the afternoon on Saturday. Then I'd lounge in bed while Dean made breakfast and mimosas. If we didn't have anywhere to be, and we often didn't, we'd lie by the pool, snack, listen to music, and talk about all the things we were going to do in life. Now we're doing those things, our dreams are coming true, and there isn't much time left over for having new dreams. Or having sex.

From the day we met, Dean had it in his head that having children would destroy our sex life. After I recovered from Liam's birth, if we missed a day of sex he was like, "Oh my God, *it's happening*!" If we have sex three times in a week, he's like, "It's happening!" Sometimes he worries that we had kids too soon, that we should have taken more time for ourselves. Well, sure. We were married for exactly two months before I got pregnant.

I think our postkid sex life is fine, but I do think about how having kids has made me less adventurous. Sometimes Dean will say, "Where's that girl I met in Ottawa?" It's true that the girl he met used to do Jägermeister shots, do the splits in the middle of the floor, or pee in a potted plant without a moment's pause. That side of me, my wild streak, is pretty much gone. The most daring thing I do now is train my son to honk my boobies, risking nothing except likely public humiliation. It used to be that I'd be out with friends, laughing and drinking, and when someone said, "Another bottle of wine?" I was like, "Sure, why not?" Being out with friends is fun, but the fun drains away when you start calculating the damage. There are children waiting for me at home. I can't be reckless. My kids need their mom. And I'm tired. Bed always sounds nice, often nicer than another glass of wine.

A couple of times Dean and I have gone to dinner and I've had some wine and gotten a little loud and funny, maybe a little crass. Dean says, "There's the old TT," and it makes me feel bad. Who is the old TT (Dean's nickname for me)? Some loud mouthed drunk girl? Is that who he misses? But I know that part of me is the girl who liked to pretend she's a stripper or dance around and do the splits and flash Dean my boobs. I liked to be silly and let loose. What happened? Then I remember that I've been pregnant for two years. Maybe when I'm back to my old body, I'll be back to my old self. Or some version of my old self. Instead of gyrating on a bar, I'll be shimmying along the monkey bars at the playground. I'll be back, but in a more family-friendly form.

In some ways I'm not that girl Dean met in Ottawa less than three years ago. I handle myself very differently. But I think that's a good thing. Whenever I'm out without the children, I'm constantly thinking about them and wanting to get back to them. They need me. They depend on me. I have to think of them first. I like my friends. I love having date nights with

Dean. But at the end of everything I want to go home and be with my family. I definitely feel that all the time.

When Dean was in his twenties he rode a motorcycle. (I know, such a stud!) It was a Yamaha FJ1200 and he rode it everywhere. It was his primary means of transportation and he was really good at riding it. But when he married his first wife, the motorcycle sat dormant in the garage. She hated it, and he finally sold it. He always talked about how much he missed it, but he never rode one or thought to buy one. The cliché is that men enter marriage with interests that are fun, maybe a little reckless, and the women make them stop. I never wanted to be that woman—the one who reels a man in, keeps him home, dampens his good time. Add to that the fact that I'm a second wife. You always hear, "My first wife wouldn't let me do this or that. My first wife didn't want to do this with me." I want to be the cool, supportive one. He liked motorcycles? So did I! He wanted to buy a motorcycle? So did I. He wanted me to ride it? I'd love to but I was very, very busy organizing toothpicks. (Although we would be cute, leathered up to cruise the streets.) When Dean's first Father's Day with Stella rolled around, I rented him a motorcycle for a week. So cool. So thoughtful. So supportive of his need for speed. Such a bad idea.

Dean had so much fun riding the motorcycle that week that before I knew what was happening, he'd bought himself a brand-new motorcycle, a 2008 Ducati SportClassic 1000 with Termignoni exhaust pipes, Dynojet Power Commander, CRG levers, and Motovation frame sliders. I don't know what any of that means, but it proves how into it he is, right? Now as for all that talk about me riding the motorcycle with him, who did we think we were fooling? I'm not a thrill seeker. I've never liked roller coasters or skiing or anything particularly fast. I may have been a little more raunchy and late-night pre-kids, but I never even pretended to do scary stuff like skydiving or scuba diving or motorcycle riding. That wasn't the old me, it wasn't the married me, and it certainly wasn't the mom me. I wanted to share Dean's life, so I went on his motorcycle with him one time. It was scary. I held on for dear life. I survived. Done.

Dean does things that my friends say they'd never let their husbands do. A midnight scuba dive. The motorcycle. And after a couple of months with the motorcycle, just riding wasn't enough for him; he started taking motorcycle *racing lessons* at a track. You know, where they go so fast around turns that the bike is practically sideways. I went to watch once. It was too scary. I can't go back. But Dean is fearless. He's a daredevil. If I got him a skydiving weekend, he'd be psyched. He'd do it all if he could. Dean's the best father I could imagine. But he doesn't worry about dying and leaving nobody to raise his children. He doesn't consider the time he spends on his hobbies as time taken away from them. Is that the difference between moms and dads?

Dean saw a TV series called *Long Way Down,* in which Ewan McGregor and his friend took a marathon motorcycle ride. Dean wanted to know if it was okay with me if he undertook a long-distance ride. I said, "Yes and no." Yes, of course I didn't want to control him. I didn't want to stifle his dreams. I'm terrified of motorcycles but I wasn't his mother. I wasn't about to stop him from owning one and using it. But no, it was not okay with me on the inside. I felt jealous. I wanted to travel too. With him. Dean said, "Why can't we do it together? Where would you want to travel?" I told him I wanted to go to Milan for Fashion Week. Dean liked that idea. We could stay in Milan, then spend a week in the countryside riding motorcycles together. Or he could ride and I could relax. It sounded amazing.

Then I said, "And the kids will come." But Dean wasn't imagining it like that. He wanted us to have some time alone. He said, "Remember you said having kids would never change us?" He was right. I didn't and I don't want to stop living our lives. What I want is to incorporate our children into our lives. The reality is that I just don't want to be away from the kids. And the reality for Dean is that Liam is a daddyholic. I sit there staring happily at the children while Liam is tugging on Dean, pulling him this way and that. It's more work for Dean.

If you don't let it get to you, figuring out the details of a life that keeps changing is the fun part. I'm not worried about the future. Whatever happens, Dean and I will find our balance. We love our children. We love each other. Time, vacations, adventures—they're all secondary to love.

Unresolved Issues

After Liam was born, it seemed like my mother might have a relationship with him. Mom started making regular dates with him. He went over to her house once a week. She read books to him and played with him. This may seem like normal grandparent behavior, but it was a great step forward for me and my mom. We had a deeply conflicted relationship, but as far as I was concerned, that didn't mean she had to have a conflicted relationship with Liam. She might not be maternal, but maybe she would end up being a wonderful grandmother. Unconditional love could skip a generation. That would make me really happy. I was excited. Being a mom was a new chapter in my life, and I was ready for it to be a new chapter in my relationship with my own mother.

Liam and Paola went over to my mom's to play once a week for all of three weeks. Paola said that my mom's friends gave

Liam lots of gifts and that she kept them for him at her house, so he'd have something to play with in the room she had for him. Then one day when they came home Paola said, "They took pictures of her with Liam." The next week my mother canceled her plans with Liam. She said she was sick. She canceled three weeks in a row, but soon the photos of her with Liam went up on her website.

Then *sTORI telling* was published, and I never heard from my mother. I knew writing about our relationship in the book was a risk. I hoped we would try to preserve our fragile peace. I hoped that, if she read it, it would help her see certain things from my perspective and lead her to understand our relationship better. I hoped that she would recognize that I didn't say anything just to be hurtful or scandalous but took what I wrote seriously and only disclosed what I felt was needed to put my story across. I hoped if she were upset we could talk about it. At the very least, I hoped that she would continue to have a relationship with Liam.

I wanted to talk to my mother about the book before it came out. I thought about it. I planned to do it. I even drafted emails in my head. But in the end I didn't do it. I couldn't. I was afraid, or angry enough to feel justified in telling the truth, or hopeful that she'd read the book and understand me better than I could explain myself in an email. A little of all of those. I didn't reach out to her, and I didn't hear from her. We never spoke directly about the book, or how she felt about what I said about her in it. We didn't fight. We didn't express our feelings.

We just didn't speak. So motherhood hasn't changed that: I'm still left guessing what's in my mother's head. And I imagine that the room she had set up for Liam, with those gifts from her friends, sits unused and ghostly.

Right after Stella was born, I ran into a friend of my mother's at the Century City Westfield Mall. She was very pleasant. We chatted a little, then she said, "You should do the right thing. It's her grandchild. She should see him." I said, "My mother is welcome to see Liam." She gave me a knowing look, like, *You know that's not true.* But it was true. I said, "She even has our babysitter Paola's phone number." She shook her head as if she could see through my lies. "But is it the same babysitter? Is it the same number?" I said, "Of course it's the same number." After that encounter I figured my mother was telling her friends that I wouldn't let her see Liam. I would always let her see him. I always hope that the situation will change. Hint, hint, Mom.

I didn't call my mother to let her know when Stella was born. We had exchanged emails when I got pregnant. Then I emailed her when I found out it was a girl, and I never heard back. She didn't come to Liam's first birthday party. And I kind of gave up after that. So not calling her when Stella was born wasn't exactly a dramatic shift in the status quo. Soon enough my mother issued a statement saying she was happy at Stella's arrival and happy that Liam had a little sister. Her statement told me that she knew I had a baby. It told me that she knew the baby's name. After all these years, we're still communicating through the press. Mom posted the photos of Stella that appeared in *OK!* magazine on her website, and, as of this writing, that's the closest she's come to meeting Stella.

How I define myself as a mother is a reaction to how I was parented. I think that's true for everyone. But as I rear my own children, I find myself attached to and sentimental about the traditions I grew up with. From the moment I gave birth to Liam, I felt a connection with my mother that I'd never known before. I hoped that feeling would grow over time, but I'm still where I was, wishing for something that may never come to light. I think about how I lost Nanny, then my father, even Mimi, and how after they were gone, I regretted not having spent enough time with them. I don't want my children to have any regrets about their grandmother. I certainly don't want them to feel like I kept them apart. I would love for them to have a relationship with her—if it's substantially different from the one I had. But I haven't stepped up to make that happen.

Children of the Gays

My relationship with my mother has never been good. That news is long out of the closet. In response I put my heart into my friendships. My friendships are the core of who I am, and a major part of who I am is Queen of the Gays. But some of my best gay friends were single. Living blissfully diaper-free lives, they were less than interested in discussing the virtues of nursing bras or whether certain teethers were made out of toxic plastics. For all the times over the years when Mehran and I have visited friends with newborn babies, I had never seen him hold an infant. It's not that he was uninterested. He was terrified that he'd drop it (he always called newborns "it"), and he'd spend the whole time trying with all his might not to bolt out of the room. Mehran and my other gays are like family to me, the family I chose, so I wanted them to be a major part of first Liam's—then Stella's—life. But I was afraid that once I had a child myself, my fag-hag status would plummet so far down that it would take me and my Christian Louboutins years to climb out of the baby ditch.

The day Liam was born, Mehran came to the hospital. For all my fears, he walked right into my hospital room and scooped Liam up. Next thing I knew he was asking the nurse to show him how to swaddle. The Guncles, Bill and Scout, are always at our house, and every time they come they bring little gifts—a monkey sippy cup, a ladybug towel. They shower our children with presents and love, like young, attractive, male grandmas. Scout and Bill are always debating how old Liam has to be before we can take him to the Abbey, which is arguably the best gay bar in Los Angeles. My position is that it's a bar, and he's a baby, and those two don't mix, to which they always respond, "But *the patio*! Babies are always welcome on patios!" I do have to admit that there's something benign about a patio. Actually, Bill and Scout aren't alone in their obsession with escorting Liam to the Abbey. There was much competition among my friends as to who gets to take Liam to his first gay bar, but now that I think about it, Liam's already been to a gay bar. He was five months old when we had the premiere party for season 2 of *Tori & Dean* at Hamburger Mary's in West Hollywood. We had a private room in the back of the bar, and Liam was in a booth, perched in his car seat, absorbing his first lesson in tolerance while the crew milled around sipping margaritas. Sorry, friends.

There is definitely a "gay watch" on Liam. Even before he

was born, Mehran was worried that Liam would be too straight to hang out with him. He was always like, "With my luck you'll have a jock son who's not into fashion and wants nothing to do with me." He imitated future teenage Liam saying "Hey, man" in a big, dumb voice.

In hopes of being an early influence, lots of my friends gave me gay-themed gifts at my baby shower. A pink onesie saying "My boyfriend's out of town for the weekend." A rock T-shirt saying "Queen" (as in the band). But despite these blatant attempts at influencing my son's sexuality (Oh, sure, they always say "It's genetic!" It's genetic until it comes to swaying my own child), the verdict so far seems to be that Liam is straight. Mehran always says he's superstraight. But every once in a while they'll catch him tiptoeing and hope springs anew.

Instead of driving my friends away, Liam, and now Stella, have added something to their lives. Mehran even has a picture of them on his desk. People think he's married (which he sort of is—to me). Of course, the manicures and shopping trips with Mehran don't happen like they used to. One Sunday when Dean was racing, Mehran came over and we had great plans for Barneys, Fred Segal, and brunch. But before we knew it, it was five p.m. and we were having dinner at Jerry's Deli with the kids. Mehran said, "What happened to our Sunday?" What happened was we'd gone to a baby store for a new monitor. We stopped by Walgreens for diapers. We fed babies. We rocked babies. We supervised naps. Now here we were at Jerry's. Meanwhile, Bill and Scout are so in love with Liam and Stella that they've started talking about adopting. I'm going to send them to swim class with Liam and feed the boy as many prunes as he'll eat right before, so they can have the classic poop-in-the-swim-diaper experience. Just so they know what to expect.

When Stella was two months old, Dean and I had to take a flight to New York for business. We were going for two days and were leaving the kids at home. Of course I started thinking about how we were going to die in the plane, and as soon as I went down that path I realized that we didn't have a will. That if we died suddenly, nobody would know what to do with our children.

Dean and I had already decided that if something ever happened to us, we wanted our friends to step in as guardians for the children. Mehran, Jenny, and the Guncles are the people who know the children best. We want Bill and Scout to be their day-to-day guardians, moving into our house and raising them. We want Mehran, who loves them just as much, to be a guardian as well. And we want Jenny, who's busy with three kids of her own, to be part of their lives. She's the most experienced, and the kids would need a woman in their lives.

The day before we left we were having brunch with Bill and Scout. After Dean put our plates on the table, we told them what we'd been thinking. I didn't know how they'd react. Two kids are a lot to throw at a couple, even if only in rare and extreme circumstances. There was a moment of silence. I looked at Dean nervously. Was this stupid? Were we asking too much? Was it stupid to feel stupid for asking? Then Bill said,

"I don't have any money, but I'd spend every last dime I have fighting your mother for those kids." I burst into tears, and I still tear up when I remember that moment. I thought, *God, there's someone who loves me so much that he'd be willing to risk everything he has to take care of my kids.*

I said to Mehran, "You're a single gay man. You're fabulous. I want you involved, but I wouldn't want you to have to give up your lifestyle."

But Mehran said, "I'd do what I had to do. I'd take the kids, move back in with my parents, and take care of them."

My friends were already like family to me, but hearing that they would do anything, they would change their lives for me—it was incredible. It filled a hole in my heart that I hadn't known was there.

By the day we were leaving, we had a plan, but we still didn't have anything on paper. When Mimi was alive, every time I flew without her I put a note in my bedside drawer saying that if my plane crashed, Isabel should have custody. I should clean out that drawer; I bet there are at least a dozen Mimi-custody documents floating around on scraps of paper in there.

So I put another note in my not-quite-legally-sanctioned bedside drawer. It said, "To Whom It May Concern: Please see that Liam and Stella are in the hands of . . ." and listed my friends. Thank God the plane didn't crash. I'm sure that miserable scrap of paper would have kept a custody battle going until the kids were high school graduates. Even so, I got on that plane knowing that my children had a family who loved them and would care for them as best they could. It gave me a sense of peace.

Just a few months later, when Dean's birthday came around, he and I spent a night at Casa del Mar, the nearby beachside hotel where we stayed when we first left our marriages. For the first time Bill and Scout stayed overnight with the kids. Patsy was there to help with Stella, but they took care of Liam completely alone. When he woke up in the middle of the night asking for "Dada," Scout gave him some water. He said, "Dada sent me." Liam drank some water and went back to sleep. The next morning Scout sent a picture of Liam having breakfast, and I burst out crying. There was Liam, happily eating a banana in his high chair with Bill lovingly gazing on. Liam was there with two people who weren't technically his family. His mom and his dad weren't there. His babysitter wasn't there. And he was fine. My little boy.

Goodnight Moon

Not long after we came home from our trip to New York, it was time to move to our new house. In the end we left Beaver Avenue without really saying good-bye. There was so much to do leading up to the move—packing, painting the kids' new rooms, setting up the TVs I continue to require in every room. And then moving day is always stressful and hectic. I meant to stop by the neighbors, but I never did. When Patsy and I put the children into the car to drive away for the last time, I thought about running over to Wally's house for a farewell hug and bringing Liam to Sam's house to say good-bye. I know they were kind people, and if we'd stayed for three or four years we would have gotten much more comfortable with one another. Time does that to people. But I never gave it a chance, and now it was too late. Still, after we moved I wanted to thank the people who I know went out of their way to make me feel welcome in my first neighborhood. I dropped off red velvet cupcakes on their doorsteps. And this time (unlike July Fourth) I wasn't doing it for credit. I wasn't doing it to prove that I fit in. I just wanted to say thank you.

The day we moved, Dean had to be on the set for a TV movie he was making. (Our crew was also filming it for *Tori & Dean*.) Filming went into the evening, and I went to visit the set with Liam, Stella, and Patsy. It got later, and the children were getting tired. Dean said, "Stella's falling asleep. It's late for Monkey. Why don't you go back home?" I stalled. The truth was that I didn't want to drive home to our new house at night without Dean. It seemed so far away, a long drive over the hill and out of L.A. But when it became clear Dean couldn't leave any time soon, I forced myself to leave.

We came home. The rooms were still full of boxes, but we'd bought some furniture from the original owner, so the living rooms were set up, and we'd made sure the beds were all ready. Patsy went to put Stella to sleep, and I brought Liam upstairs to his new bedroom. I'd covered the walls in the same fabric he'd had on Beaver Avenue to help with the transition, but Liam wasn't buying it. He wanted Dean to put him to bed. He was scared and started crying, "I 'cared. I 'cared." It was nine at night, long past his bedtime. He was overtired and in a new place, and he had a full-blown kicking, screaming, back-arching meltdown. I don't like to humor tantrums, but how could I fault him for being scared when I was feeling a little creeped out myself? I was hiding my fear with every mother fiber of my being, but maybe he'd picked up on it. I said, "Monkey, let's put on pj's and watch a movie in my bed." Ah, the magic of TV. He stopped crying.

I brought Liam into our bed and got him situated on Dean's side. I started flipping through the kids' channels and came across *Charlie and the Chocolate Factory* with Johnny Depp. I loved that book as a child and hadn't seen the Johnny Depp version, so I put it on. Fifteen seconds into the first scene I realized that this was not a good movie for a toddler. I said, "Monkey, I'm going to change the channel." Liam screamed. Okay, just a little more.

As we were watching I suddenly got spooked. We were alone in a big house. It was so quiet and dark. The alarm system hadn't been activated yet. Patsy, a mature, responsible adult, was in her room, but that didn't make me feel any better. I was here with my vulnerable young children and I didn't feel safe.

I started to have a full panic meltdown about living in this house. On Beaver Avenue I never felt scared when Dean was away. Maybe it was because I knew that if I barely whistled, Wally would come to help. Now I was stuck in this big, dark, echoey house. Had I made a terrible mistake? Was this house everything I'd never wanted? As a child in my parents' vast house I'd dreamed of moving into the cozy closet in the laundry room. I love small spaces. Why would I want this big house? What was I doing here?

Midpanic, I glanced back at *Charlie and the Chocolate Factory*. Liam was riveted by a cute scene with squirrels shelling nuts. This movie wasn't so bad after all. But then, as we watched, Veruca Salt was attacked by hundreds of squirrels. Yikes. I quickly grabbed Liam's blanket and hid the screen from him, saying, "It's funny! The squirrels are tickling her! But don't watch." Suddenly I flashed back to my mother sitting me in front of a horror movie at age four. Liam wasn't even two. I quickly turned off the TV and told him the movie was over.

I took out a book that my mother used to read me as a child. *Goodnight Moon.* It was always my favorite bedtime story. Liam and I leaned on pillows next to each other, I read the book, which bids good night, one by one, to the things in a little bunny's bedroom—the light, the red balloon, the clocks, the socks . . . Liam's eyelids got heavy. He was finally calm and peaceful, and as I comforted him, I felt comforted. It didn't escape me that I was in a big house, though not nearly as big as those I grew up in, feeling comforted—and comforting my son—with the same book that comforted me as a child. But as a parent I'd made the changes to the scene that I wanted to make. Liam and I curled up and went to sleep together.

Whatever fears I have about our new house, I have to get over them, and I will. This is a great house. It's a great area for families. The goal is for all of us to be happy, and I can't let my irrational fears stop me from doing things in my life. I'm not going to let them get in the way of my kids' lives. I'm a mom now. I have to step up. Kids have a way of forcing us to grow up. Parenting hasn't erased my fears, but it's changed the way I handle them. And maybe, just maybe, that will help me say good-bye to them, one by one.

Afterword: The Other Shoe

My twenties—my life after *90210*—was a period when everything seemed unstable. Work was unreliable. I made bad boyfriend choices. And my relationship with my family was rocky at best. I look at my life now, and I'm amazed that things have somehow miraculously sorted themselves out. I have a loving husband. I have two amazing children. I have a stepson I treasure. We have close friends who are a part of my children's lives. I'm building a career and a brand, my own mini empire. Together those people are the family that I always wanted—a family that I created for myself.

I've come far, but my life came together so quickly that sometimes I still feel like I'm waiting for the other shoe to drop. I can't believe how fortunate I am, and I worry that my perfect little dream will burst and everything will fall apart. I have to remind myself that the life I'm living isn't really a miracle. I have worked hard for what I have. I continue to work every day to sustain what we have and to make it better. But if things change, I'll weather it. I have my family and my friends to help me through it. And besides, this whole "other shoe" business—who ever said that the other shoe was a bad thing? Two shoes. Sounds good to me. Especially if they're Christian Louboutin.

It's not a coincidence that everything fell into place at the same time. As I got older I started to accept who I was. I ended my first marriage because I had to stop pretending to be someone's ideal wife. I fell in love with a man who loved me for myself. Being with Dean gave me more confidence to come to terms with my life and circumstances. When we came back from our honeymoon I decided to make *So NoTORIous,* a show that poked fun at me and my life. For thirty-some-odd years I've been trying to get away from who I was and where I'd come from. *So NoTORIous* was the first step toward accepting and embracing myself as I was and putting that out in the world. When I did so, it felt right. After that, doors started to open for me, or I started to open doors for myself.

In a baby way, I feel like I'm following in my father's footsteps. Obviously I'm not remotely where he was in terms of achievement and success, not by any standards. I'm still at the beginning. But now, like him, I know what I want to do and be. And like my dad, I understand what people want from me. I'm able to make a life out of that understanding, personally and in business. It may look like I have my hands in a lot of pots—the show, my jewelry line, my children's clothing line, our production company—but all my efforts are driven by the notion that I'm putting myself out there, I'm going by what I know and offering it to other people. For now, they seem to be interested in what I have to say. After being mocked for my role in *90210,* turned away from jobs for who I was—*that* Tori Spelling—I finally feel accepted.

Once my dad passed away there was family closure. He had kept me tied to that family. Without him there was no guilt and no strings. I felt free to go on with my life. A new family emerged (my friends, Dean) and grew (Liam, Stella). I still worried about escaping my past. But one thing I've realized about being a mother is that I don't have to figure it all out overnight. I'll make mistakes, but if I continue to be thoughtful and present, I'll notice them and try to fix them. As a mom I want always to be a work in progress. It's the best guarantee I have that I won't replicate my relationship with my mother.

My father and Nanny aren't around to be the active grandparents I always imagined for my children. When I used to look up at my father with my big brown eyes, he'd do anything for me. I know it would have been the same when Stella looked up at him with her big blue eyes. Liam looks so much like my dad that it makes me feel like my father's nearby. And I know that Nanny can see that I listened when she taught me how to be a good person, how to be the person I am today. I remember every moment of that. I know that who I am as a mom comes from what she taught me. I miss both Daddy and Nanny, while at the same time as I feel like they're still with me.

Raising normal kids in Hollywood sometimes feels like an oxymoron. Giving my kids that down-to-earth upbringing I always fantasized about is especially hard for me since I've never lived anywhere else or worked in any other business. I mean, I have a feeling I constructed all those fantasies about a "normal" childhood from seeing "normal" families on TV shows. There is no question my kids will be Hollywood kids. Liam may always prefer the weeklies to *Goodnight Moon,* and I'm sure I'll pass the fashion bug on to Stella. But with Dean, I will find a balance for them. I know what's most important: time with my kids, time as a family, time to explore the world together, make discoveries, and talk about the lessons we learn. Love shines through everything. No matter how blinding the paparazzi flashbulbs may be, I know that my children will always feel my arms around them, actually or figuratively, and they'll see beyond the superficial interference.

Liam is still a Daddy's boy. For now. A few days ago Dean took Liam and went to get Jack for the day. The boys were together from two p.m. to eight p.m. When they got home I said, "Hi, Monkey! I missed you," but Liam wouldn't even look at me. He just said, "Daddy, Daddy." I got his Goldfish crackers and said I'd open the packet for him. He said, "No! Daddy, Daddy." All week I've been putting him to bed. The first night he had a tantrum, crying, "Daddy, Daddy, my daddy." I spent forty-five minutes talking him through it. I said, "Daddy went night-night. He's sleeping. Now it's time for you to go to sleep. I love you. You're fine. You're safe." I said the same things over and over again. But there wasn't one moment when I felt tired or frustrated. (Thank you, Mimi, for teaching me patience.) Finally, he calmed down and snuggled into bed. I said, "Good night, angel. I love you."

I walked away from Liam's bedroom feeling very proud of myself. When I got to our bedroom Dean said, "That was an ordeal, right?" But no, it hadn't felt like an ordeal. I was happy to spend forty-five minutes making my child feel comfortable and safe. I couldn't imagine having anything better to do with my time. I was confident. It felt natural. I wasn't a new, inexperienced parent anymore. I was a real mother, and it made me happy to see my son growing, to see Liam realizing that he could go to sleep with me instead of Dean. I saw it as a breakthrough. I told Dean, "No, it was fine. We're adjusting a learned behavior. It takes time."

Dean and I are learning to share our parenting, to balance experience and inexperience, and to talk through the hard patches. We don't have to be on the same page every minute. No matter how busy our day is or if we're having a disagreement, we always take moments throughout the day to stop, to hug and kiss, and to tell each other how much we love each other. Dean is really good at initiating that. Our challenge is to balance the newness of our family with our different experiences. But undertaking new adventures with the wisdom and experience that life brings is what it's all about. Dean is my soul mate, and I'm always grateful to be growing a family with him.

Just the other night, Dean went to take Liam up to bed. Liam turned and said, "Mama." My heart. Oh my God! He was in Dean's arms but he wanted me. I took him, trying to be cool. I said to Dean, "Isn't this good?"

And Dean said, "My heart's breaking a little bit right now, but yes, it's good." Halfway up the stairs Liam changed his mind. He reached out for Dean. But for those first five steps he wanted his mama. There's hope for me yet.

There are worse things for my children than a Hollywood childhood. I have some fond memories of my own. I think again about the Christmas snow that my parents famously arranged to have delivered to our backyard so their Los Angeles children would have a white Christmas. I'm definitely doing it. I don't know how much it costs, but even if all I can afford is to spread bags of crushed ice across a sandbox, I'm doing it. The Christmas snow is something Jenny, Mehran, and my other friends have been hearing about for years. The snow wasn't really a family tradition; my parents only did it twice. But that extravagance—the jokes we've made about it over the years—*that* is a tradition between me and my friends. We'll have a big chuckle over doing it for our children. And I know that over the years we'll create our own traditions—simple traditions, extravagant ones, silly ones, and romantic ones. I look at my children—they're still so small—and feel grateful for the years of memories that we have ahead of us.

I spent so long wanting and trying to change my life. I've accepted and embraced "Tori Spelling," and I'm trying in my work to make the most out of being true to myself. The same goes for me as a mother. My kids may not have a normal life. I may be raising them in Mommywood. But I love them, and no matter if we're appearing on red carpets, getting the neighbors in a tizzy, or being documented in weekly magazines, love is love.

Acknowledgments

In my first book, *sTORI telling*, I thanked the friends, family, and colleagues who were instrumental in my life as I was growing up and were supportive of the woman I had become. I'm happy to say that the cast of characters hasn't changed. All of those same wonderful people still have my eternal gratitude and love!

For this book I'd like to thank the people who have been a huge part in making me the mom I am today.

Dean . . . Babe, thank you for giving me our two beautiful babies and loving us to no end. You have made me the confident wife and mother I am today, and I am hopelessly in love with you forever. You and I together have created a beautiful family and love story, my prince! You are our everything.

Mehi . . . I always knew you loved me, but the love you've shown my children has amazed me. As my gay husband you've stepped up and taken on daddy duties when needed. Who knew you would jump in to change a poopy diaper? I love you for that. I love you for all that you are to me and my family. You are eternally my Chic Rock!

Jenny . . . Thank you for being the wealth of baby knowledge that you are. I look to you as a young woman looks to her mom when she becomes a mom herself. Your guidance has been invaluable and your love for family is priceless. You are my sister, my best friend, and one *hell* of an aunt! With you my kids will never have a shortage of love and laughter.

Scout and Bill . . . Liam and Stella's Guncles! I always longed for family members who would shower my own children with love, support, and gifts. Now I have them. I tear up every time I see you with my babies and see how your love for them is so abundant and effortless. When my children are with you I feel 100 percent safe. And, with all of my irrational fears, we all know how hard it is for me to achieve that feeling of safety.

Amy and Sara . . . Thank you for being true girlfriends and sisters to me. I love that my kids have such loving aunts.

To Jennifer, Marcel, Suzanne, and Brandy . . . I love you with all my heart and am so happy that you are a part of my children's lives. Each of you has a unique personality that will indeed add to their character and true being.

Daddy and Nanny . . . Your love and guidance made me the parent I am today. I hope I have made you proud and I know

ACKNOWLEDGMENTS 241

you look down on your two beautiful grandchildren every day with smiles from above.

Jack . . . You are an amazing big brother! Liam and Stella adore you and so do I.

Mimi . . . Thank you for teaching me patience and loving me till the end. You will always be in my heart.

Uncle Danny and Aunt Kay . . . Thank you for being so good to my kids. You shower them with love and gifts and me with endless encouragement.

My dogs . . . Thanks for your patience with the kids. Tail-pulling can't be fun!

Isabel, Patsy, and Paola . . . Thank you for loving my babies as if they were your own. All three of you are dear family to us.

Dr. J . . . Thanks for bringing my two beautiful babies into this world safely, expertly, and with a few laughs along the way.

Dr. Wexler . . . Thanks for your patience, kindness, and guidance toward couple and mommywood bliss.

Dr. Sonya Gohill . . . Thank you for your amazing care of Liam and Stella and always patiently dealing with all of my questions and irrational fears.

Ruthanne . . . To call you my amazing agent doesn't do you justice; to call you my champion does. You're my wingman and my friend for life. Let's continue to build the dream together. I love you!

Gueran . . . Others crumbled, you rallied. You believed, therefore I am. Super agent, even better friend. My family is eternally grateful to you. T Bag 4 Life!

Jacob . . . You have been a great agent to Dean and me, but your friendship is beyond. We are as dedicated to you as you are to us. Fish tank or no fish tank.

Meghan and Jill . . . You helped the Little Engine That Could get to the top of the hill and now it's full steam ahead. You are amazing publicists, but your personal investment in and unbelievable dedication to me and my family has made you friends for life.

Jamie . . . You've been an amazing lawyer and friend. I know you have *big* clients, yet you still take time to be instrumental in building, executing, and protecting all of my dreams.

Oxygen . . . Thank you for being the network that believed, cultivated, and built my dream.

World of Wonder . . . Your passion and excitement make me believe in myself. Your love for my family makes you all dear friends.

Thank you to the rest of my team for your hard work and love . . . Rachael at PMK; my agents at UTA; my lawyers at Jackoway, Tyerman, Wertheimer, Austin, Mandelbaum & Morris; and Gary, Eleanor, and everyone at Kessler Schneider.

And to the key players who made this book possible . . .

Hilary Liftin . . . Once again you captured my voice to a tee. You make my book *me*. And we have fun doing it! Thank you. And ohhh, the stories I already have for our next book!

Dan Strone . . . Thanks again for making my second book a reality.

Jen Bergstrom . . . my fabulous publisher, who *so* gets me. Thank you for always believing in me and encouraging me to *rock it*!

Patrick Price . . . My talented and hilarious editor and friend. The ride with you has been amazing and it makes me want to do another book just to continue our witty email banters. You make me confident and you make me smile.

Michael Nagin . . . Thank you, my talented art director, for always letting my type-A personality be a part of the process down to the miniscule details.

Mike Rosenthal . . . Again, thank you for capturing the essence of me and my book in photographs.

Jennifer Robinson . . . Thank you for your hard work, continuing to make people aware and garner my stories great publicity.

And to Simon Spotlight Entertainment/Simon & Schuster . . . Thanks again for giving my voice a home.

This book is dedicated to Liam and Stella: my beautiful babies, my angels on earth, my greatest gifts ever, and the best part of me. I love you with all that I am.

Love, Tori